Environmental
IMPACT

D1197987

What Is the Impact of
CLIMATE CHANGE?

Craig E. Blohm

ReferencePoint
Press

San Diego, CA

For more information, contact:
ReferencePoint Press, Inc.
PO Box 27779
San Diego, CA 92198
www.ReferencePointPress.com

LIBRARY OF CONGRESS CATALOGING-IN-PUBLICATION DATA

Names: Blohm, Craig E., 1948- author.
Title: What is the impact of climate change? / by Craig E. Blohm.
Description: San Diego, CA : ReferencePoint Press, Inc., 2021. | Series:
  Environmental impact | Includes bibliographical references and index.
Identifiers: LCCN 2019053641 (print) | LCCN 2019053642 (ebook) | ISBN
  9781682828595 (library binding) | ISBN 9781682828601 (ebook)
Subjects: LCSH: Climatic changes.
Classification: LCC QC903 .B485 2021 (print) | LCC QC903 (ebook) | DDC
  363.738/74--dc23
LC record available at https://lccn.loc.gov/2019053641
LC ebook record available at https://lccn.loc.gov/2019053642

Contents

Introduction   **4**
A Deadly Heat Wave

Chapter One   **8**
Climate Change and Natural Disasters

Chapter Two   **19**
Climate Change and the Oceans

Chapter Three   **30**
Climate Change and Agriculture

Chapter Four   **41**
Climate Change and Health

Chapter Five   **52**
Climate Change Solutions

Source Notes   64
Make a Difference   69
Organizations and Websites   70
For Further Research   72
Index   74
Picture Credits   79
About the Author   80

A Deadly Heat Wave

Paris, France, is one of the world's most-visited cities. Its rich history, beautiful architecture, and charming cafés draw tourists from all over the world. Summer in Paris promises a delightful climate for strolling along historic boulevards. Yet in 2019, Paris, along with the rest of Europe, suffered a devastating heat wave that set new temperature records and resulted in numerous deaths.

On July 25, 2019, the temperature in Paris soared to 108.6°F (42.6°C), the highest ever recorded in the city's history. Tourists and Parisians alike sought relief from the heat by wading in the fountains near the Eiffel Tower. French officials recorded at least five deaths due to the extreme temperatures. Other European nations were not spared: Belgium, Germany, the Netherlands, and the United Kingdom all experienced record high temperatures.

Halfway across the globe, another heat wave had already driven temperatures up in a normally cool region. Anchorage, Alaska, which usually enjoys summer temperatures around 65° F (18° C) saw thermometers hit 90°F (32°C) on July 4. Such temperatures in Alaska are rare, yet average temperatures in the state have been steadily rising since the mid-twentieth century.

Climate Change

Paris and Anchorage are two very different cities that shared the serious consequences of extreme heat waves. This points to a disturbing trend: Earth's climate is getting hotter. July 2019 "has rewritten climate history, with dozens of new temperature records at the local, national and global level,"[1] says Petteri Taalas, the secretary-general of the World Meteorological Organization (WMO). To understand why this is happening, scientists point to greenhouse gases and resulting climate change.

Greenhouse gases are gases in the atmosphere that trap heat. The major greenhouse gases are carbon dioxide, methane, nitrous oxide, ozone, and water vapor. As sunlight enters the atmosphere, it warms the earth, allowing plant and animal life to flourish. Although some of this heat is reflected back into space, some is trapped in the atmosphere by greenhouse gases. As these gases accumulate, more heat builds up and Earth gets hotter, potentially causing harmful changes in the planet's climate. This is called the greenhouse effect.

The amount of greenhouse gases is steadily rising, and some of these gases remain in the atmosphere for hundreds, even thousands, of years.

Climate change is the long-term alteration of normal weather patterns over a large area, caused by the warming of the atmosphere. It should not be confused with weather, which is the short-term changing of atmospheric patterns in a local area. Originally known as global warming, *climate change* is now the preferred term as it more clearly represents the many results of atmospheric warming (stronger storms, altered rain patterns, droughts, and other effects). Scientists predict that if the accumulation of greenhouse gases is not slowed, the consequences of climate change—rising seas, deadly heat waves, and food shortages—could affect billions of people by the end of this century.

IMPACT FACTS

The years 2014 through 2018 were the hottest years since scientists began keeping records in 1880.

—NASA

The Human Equation

For decades, researchers have sought to determine why Earth is warming. The European and Alaskan heat waves provide a clue.

"Such intense and widespread heat waves carry the signature of man-made climate change," says Johannes Cullmann of the WMO. "This is consistent with the scientific finding showing evidence of more frequent, drawn out and intense heat events as greenhouse gas concentrations lead to a rise in global temperatures."[2] Certain human activities emit greenhouse gases into the atmosphere. These include the burning of fossil fuels (coal, oil, and natural gas) to power factories, create electricity, and run our cars and trucks. In addition, the raising of livestock, which produce carbon dioxide and methane, and the clearing of forests for agricultural use add to the greenhouse gases in the atmosphere.

Although 97 percent of climate scientists are convinced that climate change is anthropogenic—that is, created by human activity—some skeptics believe that the warming of the atmo-

Tourists and Parisians alike seek relief from the heat by wading in the fountains near the Eiffel Tower. On July 25, 2019, the temperature in Paris soared to 108°F—the highest ever recorded in the city.

sphere is a natural part of Earth's climate cycle and the planet will eventually begin to cool by itself. Even some who acknowledge the reality of climate change think that it is already too late to stop it. But despite the controversy, climate change is a problem that will not just go away.

Seeking a Solution

The Intergovernmental Panel on Climate Change (IPCC) studies the problem of climate change and provides its findings to world leaders. In 2018 the IPCC determined that the rise in Earth's temperature must be limited to 2.7°F (1.5°C) by the year 2100. Such a small rise in temperature may seem insignificant, but an increase above that level would have disastrous consequences, the panel maintains. To meet that goal, the world would need to cut carbon dioxide emissions by 70 to 95 percent by 2050 and eliminate all emissions by the end of the century. In a 2019 report, the IPCC described the scope of the problem. "For the first time ever," noted Ko Barrett, the organization's vice chair, "the IPCC has produced an in-depth report examining the furthest corners of the earth—from the highest mountains in remote polar regions to the deepest oceans. We've found that even and especially in these places, human-caused climate change is evident."[3]

Some progress toward slowing climate change is already being made. Many nations are beginning to convert their electric power from carbon-emitting sources like coal and oil to clean sources such as nuclear, wind, and solar. Likewise, electric vehicles, which produce no greenhouse gases, are becoming more affordable; one estimate predicts that 220 million electric cars could be on the roads around the world by 2030. These measures are the first small steps toward tempering climate change. But time is running out. If the citizens of Earth cannot work together to solve the climate change crisis, scientists predict the next century will bring a world of disasters from which there will be no return.

Chapter One

Climate Change and Natural Disasters

The town of Paradise is a small community of about twenty-six thousand people nestled in the foothills of Northern California's Sierra Nevada mountain range. With majestic pines and oaks surrounding the town and the benefits of a pleasant climate, Paradise has lived up to its name for more than a century. Then, in the fall of 2018, Paradise became a hell on earth.

On November 8, a wildfire sprang up about 7 miles (11 km) from Paradise. Driven by strong winds and high temperatures, the fire, which would become known as the Camp Fire, roared through the area. By the time it was brought under control eighteen days later, 153,336 acres (62,053 ha) of land were burned and more than eighteen thousand buildings were demolished. About 90 percent of Paradise was destroyed, and most of its population had to be evacuated. Eighty-five people died as a result of the Camp Fire, the worst wildfire in California's history.

It was later determined that the fire had been started by a spark from an electrical power line. But there was another factor that contributed to the destructiveness of the Camp Fire: the effects of climate change.

Growing Wildfires

The western United States is particularly vulnerable to wildfires due to its climate of warm, dry summers. According to Park Williams, a bioclimatologist at Columbia University, "In pretty much every single way, a perfect recipe for fire is just kind of written in California. Nature creates the perfect conditions for fire, as long as people are there to start the fires. But then climate change, in a few different ways, seems to also load the dice toward more fire in the future."[4]

As temperatures rise due to climate change, areas that are usually moist and cool, such as forests, dry out and become more vulnerable to fires. Changes in rainfall patterns contribute to the increased risk of wildfires, as does the earlier melting of mountain snow in spring, which leads to soil drying out earlier in the year and remaining dry longer. These factors can affect

Pictured are the remains of a charred home in Paradise, California. In 2018, 90 percent of the town was destroyed by the worst wildfire in California's history.

the duration and extent of wildfires. A 2017 study published in the *PLOS ONE* scientific journal predicts that by 2039 the average area destroyed by wildfires will increase by more than 500 percent due to climate change. Climate change also affects the impact of lightning, one of the major triggers of wildfires, by increasing the frequency of strikes.

In the United States, wildfires cost billions of dollars each year; financial losses in California's Camp Fire hit a record $16 billion. But the United States is not the only victim of increased wildfire activity due to climate change. Wildfires can occur almost anywhere on Earth where there is sufficient fuel to burn. "The most noted areas on Earth for wildfire," says natural resources consultant Steve Nix, "include the vegetated areas of Australia, Western Cape of South Africa and throughout the dry forests and grasslands of North America and Europe."[5]

In 2019, wildfires began burning in the Amazon rain forest in South America. The fires were set by farmers seeking to create more pastureland and loggers harvesting timber for houses, furniture, and other uses. The Amazon rain forest spans parts of nine South American countries, covering 2.1 million square miles (5.5 million km^2). The impact of turning such a large forest into a dry grassland will add to global climate change. The rain forest acts as a carbon dioxide "sink," meaning its vegetation stores the gas and keeps it from escaping into the atmosphere. Without this storage effect, more carbon dioxide is released into the atmosphere, adding to the growing concentration of greenhouse gases. The Amazon sink effect normally prevents some 2 billion tons (1.8 billion t) of carbon dioxide from entering the atmosphere each year. However, the amount of carbon dioxide absorbed by the sink has been decreasing, and it has diminished by about one-third since around 2005.

IMPACT FACTS

In 2018, natural disasters cost US businesses about $160 billion.

—Jim Foerster of *Forbes*

The Cost of Climate Change

When Hurricane Dorian finally moved away from the Bahamas and out into the open ocean, it left a path of destruction in its wake. Property damage estimates have ranged from $1.5 billion to $6.5 billion. As happened in the Bahamas, one huge storm can be enormously costly. Many huge storms—or a mix of storms and other weather events made more extreme by climate change—can be even more costly. Between 2016 and 2018, extreme weather events in the United States cost the nation more than $450 billion.

Experts warn that those costs will only rise if no action is taken. But they have also noted that the measures needed to reduce climate change will also require a huge financial output. A 2018 report by the Intergovernmental Panel on Climate Change estimates that between 2018 and 2035, the world must invest $2.4 trillion per year in clean energy. By 2050, the annual investment would need to be $3.5 trillion.

No matter which path the world takes at this point, climate change will have a high price tag.

A Brazilian study predicts that between 30 and 60 percent of the Amazon rain forest could eventually become dry savanna due to climate change, creating an ecological disaster.

Climate Change and Hurricanes

Although fire can be a deadly natural force, so can the wind and rain associated with tropical storms. Around the world, 2005 was a disastrous year for tropical storms. More than two dozen hurricanes (also called cyclones or typhoons, depending on their geographic location) devastated many areas of the globe. Of these, Hurricane Katrina was one of the most catastrophic in terms of lives lost and property destroyed. When Katrina hit the southern coast of the United States, more than eighteen hundred people died, and property damage reached $125 billion. In 2017 another huge storm, Hurricane Harvey, smashed into the southern US coast, causing damage equal to that caused by Katrina twelve years earlier.

Scientists have struggled with the question of whether climate change played a part in creating these devastating storms, and how it will affect future storms. It is already clear that climate change is having an effect on global weather patterns, and these patterns will continue to be altered in the future, reports Climate Central, a nonprofit science and journalism organization. "Based on their understanding of how the climate system works, scientists expect that a warming Earth will see more and more episodes of weather extremes such as droughts, floods, heat waves, and severe storms,"[6] the organization contends.

The most severe storms are hurricanes, which form over tropical oceans. Hurricanes need warm ocean waters, at temperatures of at least 80°F (27°C), to form. As these waters evaporate, they cause water vapor to rise into the lower atmosphere. Clouds form as the humid air rises, and winds begin to create the familiar rotating pattern of these storms. When wind speeds reach 74 miles per hour (119 kmh), such a storm is officially classified as a hurricane. Many hurricane clouds can reach a height of 50,000 feet (15,240 m) and a diameter of 125 miles (210 km).

As climate change continues, the temperature of the ocean's waters will rise, creating more destructive hurricanes. "With warmer oceans caused by global warming," warns James B. Elsner of Florida State University's Department of Geography, "we can expect the strongest storms to get stronger."[7] And it will not take much of a rise in ocean temperature to create problems: just a 1°F (0.56°C) increase in temperature can raise a hurricane's wind speed by up to 20 miles per hour (32 kmh). When a hurricane makes landfall, it leaves the warm ocean waters and begins to cool, losing much of its energy. But it can still cause widespread destruction on land, including torrential rains and tornadoes.

Winds also propel hurricanes as they move across the ocean. The forward speed of a typical hurricane can vary from around 16 miles per hour (26.7 kmh) to over 30 miles per hour (48.3 kmh), depending on the latitude in which it is located. Climate scientists have observed a trend in hurricane movement over the last several decades: sometimes a hurricane will slow to as little as 1 mile per hour (1.6 kmh) or stop moving forward altogether. When this happens, destruction of property and

IMPACT FACTS

Each year since 2000, some 72,400 wildfires have destroyed about 7 million acres (2.8 million ha) in the United States.

—Congressional Research Service

danger to life escalate in the areas below the storm. A slow-moving hurricane, says meteorologist Adam Douty, "makes the flooding worse, you have continued battering with the wind so it has time to weaken structures, and once they're weakened it could damage them further."[8] In September 2019, Hurricane Dorian stalled over the Bahamas, its winds and rain intensified by its stationary position. At least sixty-three deaths were reported, along with thirteen hundred people missing and seventy thousand left homeless. The Abaco Islands in the northwest Bahamas looked like a war zone in the aftermath of Dorian. Cars and boats were tossed around like toys, and buildings were crushed. Bahamian prime minister Hubert Minnis said, "The devastation is unprecedented and extensive."[9]

Hurricane Dorian is an example of what the future could hold if climate change is not halted. Climate scientists acknowledge that rising temperatures have an effect on storms, and although they may not affect the frequency of hurricanes, they will increase the intensity of these storms. In a summary of research on climate change and hurricanes, the Geophysical Fluid Dynamics Laboratory, a part of the National Oceanic and Atmospheric Administration, found that "it is likely that greenhouse warming will cause hurricanes in the coming century to be more intense globally and have higher rainfall rates than present-day hurricanes."[10]

Extreme Rainfall

Hurricanes fall into a category of study that climate scientists call extreme weather events. Heat waves, droughts, tornadoes, floods, and severe rainstorms all fall into this category. According to the Third National Climate Assessment report issued under the auspices of the US Global Change Research Program, climate change is making these weather events worse. The organization writes, "Climate change is already affecting the American people in far-reaching ways. Certain types of extreme weather events with links to climate change have become more frequent and/or intense, including prolonged periods of heat, heavy downpours, and, in some regions, floods and droughts."[11] Likewise, a 2019 survey by Carbon Brief, a climate science website based in the United Kingdom, found that 68 percent of all extreme weather

Trouble on the Zambezi River

Victoria Falls, the world's largest waterfall, is situated on the Zambezi River between the countries of Zambia and Zimbabwe. It has long been a popular destination for travelers who visit southern Africa. But drought is affecting the Zambezi, and that is having a detrimental impact on this spectacular natural wonder.

A prolonged drought in Zambia and Zimbabwe has dropped the level of the upper Zambezi, and that has brought Victoria Falls to its lowest level in two decades. Where water normally flows over the falls, now only barren rock is often visible. Although this has hurt tourism, which is a large part of the local economy, it has had other negative impacts. For instance, the Kariba Dam is situated below the falls and generates electricity for the region. With less water flowing, power generation has been reduced, creating periodic electric outages that can sometimes last for twelve hours. Likewise, fish is a staple of the local diet, but the river's fishing grounds have all but dried up, leaving fishermen to seek other sources of income.

In October 2019, President Edgar Lungu of Zimbabwe tweeted a photograph of Victoria Falls, showing a small trickle of water where a huge torrent normally flows. It is a reminder, Lungu warned, of what the country stands to lose if climate change is allowed to continue on its present course.

events recorded in its study occurred more often or were made worse by human-created climate change.

Increased rainfall is one impact that climate change has on Earth's weather. As the temperature of the atmosphere increases, the warmer air can hold more moisture. This larger volume of water vapor increases the severity of the rainfall. Weather researcher Dim Coumou notes that "the scientific community is coming to a consensus that extreme rainfall . . . is increasing in frequency over most land areas."[12] Of course, rain is necessary to grow crops, to provide drinking water for animals and humans, and to keep lakes and rivers full. The natural patterns of precipitation that occur in various parts of the world determine the intensity, frequency, and amount of rain. When those patterns are altered, the result can be too much, or not enough, rain in a particular geographic area, resulting in a disturbance of agriculture, industry, and other human activities.

In August 2018, torrential rains hit the state of Kerala on the southwest coast of India, resulting in the worst flood in nearly one hundred years. The flooding affected twenty-six hundred villages in the state, resulting in 483 deaths and forcing as many as three hundred thousand people to relocate to relief camps. July and August are usually the months when monsoons (seasonal winds) bring rainfall to India. Although the populace has usually been able to predict and prepare for these storms, weather patterns appear to be changing. "A meteorological unpredictability is looming large over the entire south India," says Gopakumar Cholayil, a climatologist at Kerala Agricultural University, "and it is more visible in Kerala and environmental hotspots such as the Nilgiris and Kodagu. Global warming is the main culprit, and in all likelihood, the floods will be followed by a severe drought."[13]

Increasing Droughts

In what may seem a cruel twist of fate, six months after the devastating rains hit Kerala, the state suffered a severe drought. The rivers that had been swollen from rainfall retreated, leaving a parched landscape behind. Droughts such as the one in Kerala rank second in environmental economic impact, according to the Union of Concerned Scientists: "Global climate change affects a variety of factors associated with drought. There is high confidence that increased temperatures will lead to more precipitation falling as rain rather than snow, earlier snow melt, and increased evaporation."[14]

A 2019 study by scientists at California's Lawrence Livermore National Laboratory (LLNL) reported that greenhouse gases have been affecting the global risk of longer and more severe droughts since 1900. The scientists examined historical evidence such as tree rings, which give a picture of the pattern of wet and dry periods caused by greenhouse gases at various stages of a tree's

In August 2018, torrential rains hit the state of Kerala on the southwest coast of India, resulting in the worst flood in nearly one hundred years.

growth. The scientists discovered evidence of human activity—which they called a "fingerprint"—on droughts as early as the beginning of the twentieth century. "By demonstrating a human fingerprint on droughts in the past," says LLNL climate scientist Paul Durack, "this study provides evidence that human activities will continue to influence droughts in the future, and we're already seeing the influence today."[15]

With droughts expected to worsen in the decades ahead, the impact on populations in affected areas will likely include reduced food supply, more health problems, a heightened risk of wildfires, and farms destroyed or yielding smaller harvests. Even now, farmers are feeling the effects of climate change. Alabama cotton farmer John DeLoach comments, "Cotton crops should be a thousand pounds, some are going to 300 pounds."[16]

Heating Up

Perhaps the clearest evidence of a warming planet caused by climate change is the increase in the occurrence and duration of heat waves around the globe. As experienced in Europe and Alaska during the summer of 2019, worldwide temperatures are rising, and they are doing so at a troubling rate. "By 2050," reports climate journalist Doyle Rice, "hundreds of U.S. cities could see an entire month each year with heat index temperatures above 100 degrees if nothing is done to rein in global warming."[17] The heat index measures both temperature and humidity to better ascertain how hot it actually feels to the human body.

Heat waves are the deadliest weather events, causing more deaths than hurricanes, tornadoes, and floods. The people most at risk are children, the elderly, people with serious health conditions that require medication, and people living or working in places that are not air-conditioned.

Extreme heat waves and other weather events are further warning signs of what the future holds if climate change is not reined in. Hurricane Dorian, the Camp Fire, and the Kerala floods all owed their ferocity, at least in part, to the warming of the planet. Although people cannot stop these natural disasters from happening, they can work to ensure that these events do not worsen due to human activity.

Chapter Two

Climate Change and the Oceans

On August 18, 2019, a group of about one hundred people hiked up a volcano named Ok in western Iceland to attend one of the most unusual funeral services ever held. The trek took two hours over rocky, barren ground and ended at the top of the volcano. Dressed in winter jackets against the raw Icelandic weather, the hikers gathered to say farewell to a familiar friend: a glacier known as Okjökull.

Thousands of years old, Okjökull (Icelandic for "Ok Glacier") once covered 6 square miles (16 km^2). Yet by 2014 it had retreated so much that glaciologist Oddur Sigurdsson of the Icelandic Meteorological Office declared it extinct. To Iceland's scientists and climate activists, identifying the cause of the demise of Ok, as the glacier was commonly known, was simple: it was a victim of climate change.

At the end of the ceremony, a plaque was placed on the mountain as a message to future generations. It reads, "Ok is the first Icelandic glacier to lose its status as glacier. In the next 200 years, all our glaciers are expected to follow the same path. This monument is to acknowledge that we know what is happening and know what needs to be done. Only you know if we did it."[18]

Around the world, glaciers will continue to melt due to climate change. The impacts of this melting ice include a shortage of freshwater, more greenhouse gases in the atmosphere, and—perhaps most devastating—a rise in sea levels and flooding that can endanger the lives and livelihoods of millions of people.

Glaciers and Ice Sheets

Water covers about 71 percent of Earth's surface, giving the planet the bright blue color that astronauts have observed and photographed while in space and on the surface of the moon. There are an estimated 332.5 million cubic miles (1.4 trillion km³) of water on Earth, 97 percent of which is saltwater in the world's oceans; the remaining 3 percent is freshwater, most of which is frozen in glaciers and ice sheets. With such a small percentage of water found in these locations, it may be surprising that glaciers and ice sheets can have a profound effect on Earth's vast oceans. But when they are impacted by climate change, they can turn the oceans into a deadly force that can wreak havoc on the civilized world.

Around the world, glaciers will continue to melt due to climate change. One big impact of this melting ice is a rise in sea levels and flooding that might endanger the lives and livelihoods of millions of people.

Glaciers form when snow in a particular place is compressed over a long period, allowing the snow to harden into ice. About one-tenth of Earth's total land area is covered by glaciers left over from the last ice age, which ended about twelve thousand years ago. Ice sheets are large glaciers that cover at least 20,000 square miles (51,080 km^2) of land area. Ice sheets smaller than that are called ice caps and are usually found on mountaintops and at the North and South Poles. Today, Earth's major ice sheets are located in Antarctica and Greenland. In the Arctic, sea ice, which forms on oceans rather than land, helps keep the polar region cool and provides an important curb on climate change.

Rising Seas of Destruction

Glaciers, ice sheets, and sea ice do what ice naturally does when the temperature goes up: they melt. All of that melted ice goes into the world's oceans, causing their levels to rise. A 2016 study headed by climatologist James Hansen, a professor in the Department of Earth and Environmental Sciences of Columbia University in New York, highlighted the impact of climate change on the oceans:

> If the ocean continues to accumulate heat and increase melting of . . . ice shelves of Antarctica and Greenland, a point will be reached at which it is impossible to avoid large-scale ice sheet disintegration with sea level rise of at least several meters. The economic and social cost of losing functionality of all coastal cities is practically incalculable.[19]

Over the centuries, humans naturally settled near the sea to take advantage of its opportunities for fishing and seafaring. Coastal cities are now found all over the globe. About 40 percent of the world's population lives within 62 miles (100 km) of a coastline, in cities or smaller communities. This means that some 3.1 billion people could be at risk of the effects of rising sea levels. In the United States, many large and medium cities, including New York City; Miami; Atlantic City, New Jersey; and Charleston, South Carolina, are at risk should sea levels dramatically rise. New York, for example, would experience serious economic and humanitarian consequences. "There's coastal real estate at risk," says Daniel Zarrilli, the senior director of climate policy for New York City, "consequences to job creation, and the natural impact of climate on the lowest income residents in New York City. . . . It's pretty profound when you think about the types of economic impacts we'll see from that. And it will be disruptive."[20] Water treatment plants and power stations are at risk for flooding, as are New York's airports and subway tunnels. Floodwaters would likely damage stores and offices, leading to business interruption and property destruction.

The risk to coastal areas is not only an American problem but also a global one. Bangladesh; Guangzhou, China; the Maldives; the Netherlands; and Nova Scotia, Canada, are all coastal regions in danger. Many people living along these threatened coastlines are poor and have few resources to cope with such a disaster.

IMPACT FACTS

If every glacier and ice cap melted, sea levels would rise 230 feet (70 m), flooding every coastal city on Earth.

—US Geological Survey

"Tuvalu Is Sinking"

Approximately halfway between Hawaii and Australia in the South Pacific Ocean lies Tuvalu, a nation made up of nine islands and atolls. It is the fourth-poorest country in the world, with more than a quarter of its population living in poverty. But poverty is not the only problem facing the islands' 11,600 inhabitants. With an average height above sea level of 9.8 feet (3 m) and a maximum of 15 feet (4.6 m), Tuvalu may become one of the first countries to suc-

cumb to rising oceans due to climate change. "The sea is eating all the sand," says Tuvalu resident Leitu Frank. "Before, the sand used to stretch out far, and when we swam we could see the sea floor, and the coral. Now, it is cloudy all the time, and the coral is dead. Tuvalu is sinking."[21]

As a culture based on farming and fishing, the Tuvaluans produce practically no greenhouse gases. But they are nevertheless at risk for the effects of climate change produced by the industrial nations of the world. Rising seas are causing coastal erosion in Tuvalu. A 2011 study reported that sea levels had been rising 0.2 inches (5 mm) per year since 1993, and it projected the rise to reach 0.28 to 0.71 inches (7 to 18 mm) by 2030. Tuvalu's groundwater has been contaminated by saltwater from the ocean, creating a shortage of freshwater and forcing farmers to rely solely on rainfall to irrigate their crops. Heat-related illnesses are also on the rise.

The government of Tuvalu has initiated a program called the Tuvalu Coastal Adaptation Project to reduce the impact of climate

Climate scientists know that the world's ice is melting. How they know this is not just guesswork; they use the latest scientific tools to measure and track the melting rate of glaciers, sea ice, and ice sheets.

The process of measuring ice on Earth actually begins in space. Since 1978 the National Aeronautics and Space Administration (NASA) has been using satellites to observe sea ice and monitor its size. NASA data confirms that there has been a decline in the amount of ice since 2002. NASA's geographic satellite Landsat 8 orbits 438 miles (705 km) above Earth. It employs an array of visual and thermal infrared sensors to collect data from Earth and transmit it to scientists on the ground. Images from Landsat 8, along with data from previous Landsat missions, provide a time-lapse record of retreating glaciers over a period of years.

The latest satellite for observing ice is the Ice, Cloud, and Land Elevation Satellite-2 (ICESat-2). Launched in 2018, its three-year mission is to measure Earth's ice using ultra-precision lasers that pulse ten thousand times a second. ICESat-2 will collect information on the annual change in height of the Greenland and Antarctic ice sheets to within 0.16 inches (4 mm). Using this data, scientists will be able to calculate the thickness of the ice and determine how much it is eroding.

change on the islands. The project, which includes constructing sea walls, placing boulders and sandbags in strategic locations along the coast, and creating artificial beaches, is projected to be completed by 2024.

Some Tuvaluans, however, feel they cannot wait for the government project to bear fruit. Many are planning to move (or have already moved) to other South Pacific islands to escape their homeland's apparently inevitable destruction. Enna Sione plans to immigrate soon to New Zealand with her family. "The weather has really, extremely changed," she says. "Sometimes I feel scared of the ocean. Maybe one time Tuvalu will disappear. From what I can see a lot is already gone. I think one day we will disappear."[22]

Endangered Polar Bears

Although humans can understand the forces behind climate change and work toward slowing its progress, animals have no choice but to adapt to their changing environment. Keeping up with that change is becoming more difficult for many species. An iconic photograph of a polar bear has become a symbol of the plight of these magnificent creatures and all animals affected by climate change.

The photograph shows a polar bear standing on a piece of floating sea ice not much bigger than the bear itself, surrounded by the vast Arctic Ocean. Polar bears use such ice floes as platforms for hunting seals and fish, but with climate change raising the water's temperature, more ice melts and leaves fewer places from which to hunt. Climate scientists estimate that Arctic sea ice is disappearing at the rate of about 14 percent every ten years. Travel writer Henry Wismayer, who flies thousands of miles a year for his job, realizes the individual's responsibility for contributing to climate change. "My flights alone," he says, "have accounted for some 90 tons of carbon emissions, enough to melt about 260 square meters of polar sea ice. I have melted a tennis-court-size chunk of the Arctic all on my own."[23]

Fewer ice floes means that polar bears must swim farther to find suitable hunting grounds and must rest during the hunt. That is taking a toll on the animals. Blaine Griffen, a biologist at Brigham Young University in Provo, Utah, has spent years studying the feeding habits of polar bears. He states,

> Bears can more than double their body weight during the springtime foraging season when they hunt seals on the ice. As the sea ice melts earlier and earlier, polar bears are forced to swim more and more, both in frequency and distance, to reach seal populations. The time they have to forage is getting cut short and this has huge energetic costs.[24]

Polar bears use ice floes for hunting seals and fish, but rising average temperatures means more ice melts, which leaves fewer places from which to hunt. This is taking a toll on the animals.

With fewer places to hunt, some polar bears abandon the dwindling ice floes to forage for food in inhabited areas on land. This, however, may bring hungry polar bears into populated areas, which can result in attacks on humans and people killing the polar bears in self-defense. Between 2010 and 2014, the number of polar bear attacks increased due to a scarcity of summer sea ice. During that time, fifteen polar bear attacks on humans were recorded, the most ever in a four-year span. "A bear's still got to eat," says Geoff York, the senior director of conservation at the nonprofit Polar Bears International. "They're more likely to try new things, and sometimes, that might be us."[25]

Penguins at Risk

At the opposite end of the world, Antarctica is home to the emperor penguin. This flightless aquatic bird can reach almost 4 feet (1 m) in height and weigh around 80 pounds (36 kg). Penguins have endeared themselves to humans because of the comical way they walk, their swimming prowess, and their black-and-white, tuxedo-like coloring. But although humans may enjoy observing penguin antics, they are also endangering the birds through climate change.

The world's oceans have absorbed more than 90 percent of the heat from anthropogenic warming since the 1970s. As the oceans absorb heat from the atmosphere, they grow warmer. This change in temperature thus reduces ice and disrupts the ocean's delicate ecosystem.

In Antarctica, which is home to 12 million penguins—including emperor, Adélie, and chinstrap species—such increases in ocean temperature have devastating impacts. A 2014 study conducted by the Woods Hole Oceanographic Institution (WHOI) in Massachusetts concluded that climate change will reduce the population of penguin colonies in Antarctica, some as much as 50 percent by the end of the century. "The role of sea ice is complicated," notes Stephanie Jenouvrier, a WHOI biologist. "But too little ice reduces the habitat for krill, a critical food source for emperor penguins."[26]

Krill are shrimp-like crustaceans that are eaten by penguins, seals, fish, sea birds, and even the giant blue whale. Although an average krill measures about 0.4 to 0.8 inches (1 to 2 cm) in length, they can form a biomass reaching a density of 30,000 krill per 35 cubic feet (1 m^3). Krill eat microscopic algae that live on the underside of Antarctic ice. As climate change reduces the amount of ice, there is less area for the algae to grow, and, in turn, the krill have less to eat. The krill population thus decreases, imperiling the penguins and other animals that rely on these tiny crustaceans for sustenance.

Threatened Coral

Like krill, coral is a living organism, and it too is affected by climate change. As the oceans heat up, they can absorb more carbon dioxide and thus become more acidic. Normally, seawater is slightly alkaline. When carbon dioxide is absorbed by water, it forms carbonic acid, which raises the acidity level of the water. Studies show that ocean acidification is happening ten times faster than Earth has experienced during the last 300 million years. This rapid acidification results in harm to coral and other sea life.

Vacationers who snorkel in clear, tropical waters are delighted by the striking colors of coral reefs not far below the surface. The bright colors are not natural to the organism. They are caused by algae that live in a symbiotic, or interdependent, relationship with the coral. The algae, called zooxanthellae, provide the coral with nutrients; in turn, the coral gives the zooxanthellae a protective environment and the nutrients they need for photosynthesis. But changing temperature and acidity puts stress on the coral. To

The Beginning of Extinction

Polar bears and penguins are not the only animals that may be facing extinction due to climate change. Many species around the world are in danger of disappearing as their environments are changed by higher temperatures, stronger storms, and rising seas. For one small mammal living on an island near Australia, the end has already come.

Scientists have declared the Bramble Cay melomys the first species to become extinct because of climate change. A rodent measuring about 5.9 to 6.5 inches (14.9 to 16.5 cm) long, the Bramble Cay melomys was discovered by sailors in 1845 on a small coral island of the Great Barrier Reef. At that time, the mouse-like rodents were abundant on the island, largely subsisting on vegetation growing there. By 1998, however, surveys tallied less than one hundred of the rodents, and in 2004 only a dozen could be found. After researchers had not seen even one melomys on the island for more than a decade, the species was declared officially extinct in 2016.

Why did the Bramble Cay melomys disappear? Researchers determined that rising sea levels due to climate change had reduced the rodent's habitat to such an extent that it could no longer find enough food or shelter to live. The fate of the Bramble Cay melomys should be a warning of the importance of protecting animals endangered by climate change; once they are gone, it is a loss that cannot be restored.

conserve the nutrients that are normally shared with the zooxanthellae, the coral expels the algae. Without the zooxanthellae, the coral loses its color and turns white, a process known as coral bleaching. Without the nutrients that the zooxanthellae provide the coral in return, the coral can die, depriving the world of a living organism that helps protect coastal areas from erosion, supports the fishing and tourism industries, and provides compounds used in making medicines for numerous human diseases.

Indeed, the world's oceans provide an abundance of benefits for the good of humankind. They absorb carbon dioxide and produce oxygen, feed billions of people worldwide, are essential for the global transportation of goods, and add nearly $300 billion annually to the US economy alone through ocean-dependent industries. Climate change's negative impacts threaten the world's oceans and the people and wildlife that depend upon them.

IMPACT FACTS

The mass bleaching of coral, which occurred once every twenty-five to thirty years before 1980, now occurs every six years due to climate change.

—American Meteorological Society

Chapter Three

Climate Change and Agriculture

A churning black cloud rolled over the Oklahoma panhandle, turning day into night and obscuring the landscape for miles around. It was April 14, 1935, a day that would come to be known as Black Sunday. From Texas to Canada, North America was in the midst of the Dust Bowl, a period of severe dust storms that caused destruction and economic ruin for a decade—and was caused primarily by human action.

When farmers migrated to the Great Plains during the late nineteenth century, they had limited knowledge about the climate and soil composition of the region. They replaced hardy prairie grasses with crops of corn and wheat that were less suitable to the land. When a long period of droughts came, these crops failed, and the soil began to erode. Winds whipped up great dust storms of loose dirt that covered everything and forced millions of people to abandon their farms. It took years after the droughts ended to restore agriculture to the Great Plains.

Today there are fears that the world may be headed for a new dust bowl. In August 2019 the IPCC issued a special report entitled *Climate Change and Land* that detailed the problem of desertification, which is the degradation of arable lands into barren deserts. According to the report, farmland today is losing more soil than it can create. The IPCC writes,

Soil erosion from agricultural fields is estimated to be currently 10 to 20 times . . . to more than 100 times . . . higher than the soil formation rate. Climate change exacerbates land degradation, particularly in low-lying coastal areas, river deltas, drylands and in permafrost areas. . . . In 2015, about 500 million people lived within areas which experienced desertification between the 1980s and 2000s. . . . People living in already degraded or desertified areas are increasingly negatively affected by climate change.[27]

The Dust Bowl of the 1930s was an example of desertification, and its total cost to the US economy was an estimated $1 billion (more than $15 billion in 2019 dollars). A new dust bowl would threaten food production, worsen worldwide hunger, and endanger human health. Just as poor agricultural practices caused the first dust bowl, climate change may foster a second one.

During the 1930s, North America was in the midst of the Dust Bowl, a period of severe dust storms that caused destruction and economic ruin for a decade—and was caused primarily by human action.

Food Insecurity

Hunger is one of the most devastating consequences of climate change. Roshni is a child who lives in the state of Madhya Pradesh in India. Roshni weighs 6.3 pounds (2.9 kg), but her weight should be closer to 10 pounds (4.5 kg). About 60 percent of children in Madhya Pradesh are malnourished. Although India has made recent strides in alleviating poverty, Roshni is one of 195 million people in the nation who do not have enough food to eat.

In a world of 7.7 billion people, 820 million—more than 10 percent of the world's population—go to bed hungry every night. These people are termed *food insecure*, which means they have no reliable access to nutritious food due to agricultural practices or social or economic conditions. Most food-insecure populations are in poverty-stricken developing nations; these nations are also the most susceptible to the effects of climate change. However, 40 million Americans are also food insecure.

Population growth studies indicate that by 2050, there will be 9.8 billion people in the world, which will result in a 70 percent increase in demand for food. As climate change increasingly impacts agriculture, that demand is likely to become more difficult to meet. "The main way that most people will experience climate change," says Tim Gore, the head of policy, advocacy, and research for the charitable organization Oxfam, "is through the impact on food—what they eat, how it's grown, the price they pay for it, and the availability and choice they have."[28]

About 37 percent of Earth's land is devoted to agriculture; of that, 77 percent is used for raising livestock and 23 percent for growing crops. The quantity and quality of the food produced by farming depends on many factors. Among these are the amount of rainfall an area receives, the quality of soil in which crops are planted, the availability of fertilizer, and the effective control of pests. Although these conditions combine to create ideal conditions for agriculture in many regions of the world, farmers in other places toil to produce a subsistence living from the land. Climate change affects both of these situations in different ways.

Farming and Climate Change

A significant factor that affects agriculture is temperature. Each crop has an ideal temperature range for the best yield. Corn, for example, grows best when the temperature is between 64°F and 91°F (18°C and 33°C). Wheat thrives at temperatures between 70°F and 75°F (21°C and 24°C). Above these temperatures, crops can develop heat stress, which results in smaller harvests. For example, if climate change remains unchecked, by the end of the century US corn production could be reduced by almost 50

A New Diet for Cows

Cows are an important part of the food chain. They provide milk and other dairy products, meat, leather, and livelihoods for millions of people around the world. But cows also produce something that damages the environment: methane. When a cow burps or passes gas, methane is released into the atmosphere, adding to the total amount of greenhouse gases that are responsible for climate change. Agricultural scientists have found a way to reduce these methane emissions, and it hinges on a cow's diet.

Researchers at the University of California, Davis, experimented with a species of red seaweed known as *Asparagopsis* that had reduced the amount of methane in artificial cow stomachs. They then tried it on the real thing. When mixed with a cow's feed at a concentration of 0.5 percent, the seaweed lowered methane emissions by 26 percent. A concentration of the seaweed at 1 percent reduced the methane by an impressive 67 percent. The seaweed had no observable effect on the amount or taste of the milk the cows produced.

Although these results are promising, growing enough *Asparagopsis* to feed the world's 1.5 billion cattle would be a difficult if not impossible task. Still, as long as cows continue to expel gas, scientists will search for a way to make the process as environmentally friendly as possible.

Corn grows best when the temperature is between 64°F and 91°F. Above these temperatures, corn crops can develop heat stress, which results in smaller harvests.

percent. Smaller harvests mean fewer people can get the nutritious food they need for a healthy life. Pauline Scheelbeek, the lead author of a 2018 study on climate change and the food supply, describes the problem of smaller agricultural yields:

> Vegetables and legumes are vital components of a healthy, balanced and sustainable diet, and nutritional guidelines consistently advise people to incorporate more vegetables and legumes into their diet. Our new analysis suggests, however, that this advice conflicts with the potential impacts of environmental changes that will decrease the availability of these important crops unless action is taken.[29]

The length of the growing season also affects the success or failure of crops. A growing season is the period—generally between the last frost of spring and the first frost of autumn—

during which crops can be successfully grown. In some regions the growing season is around ninety days; in others, it can last all year. Climate change alters growing seasons differently in various regions of the world. In the northern latitudes, nations such as Canada and Russia as well as some countries in northern Europe will see longer growing seasons and milder temperatures, which will benefit their agricultural industries. Although this can lead to more abundant crops for northern farmers, it would not offset the effects of climate change occurring in the southern latitudes. Africa, India, and parts of South America will experience more prolonged droughts, soil erosion, and poor crop yields. In southern Asia, about two-thirds of the population makes its living in agriculture. A 2018 study on climate change by the World Bank warns that, globally, there is "a significant risk of high-temperature thresholds being crossed that could substantially undermine food security globally in a 4°C [warmer] world."[30]

Along with providing food, farms also help fight climate change. Just as the Amazon rain forest acts as a sink to store carbon dioxide and keep it from escaping into the atmosphere, so does farmland. The top 3 feet (0.9 m) of all the soil in the world contains three times as much carbon, some 2.5 billion tons (2.3 billion t), as there is in Earth's atmosphere. With so much of the planet's land area devoted to agriculture, farmland has become an important carbon sink. Plants remove carbon from the air through photosynthesis; when the plants die and decay, the carbon is stored in the soil. But modern agricultural practices are hindering the ability of the earth to store carbon. The Carbon Cycle Institute, a nonprofit organization dedicated to reversing climate change through new farming techniques, says that the use of tractors, allowing

IMPACT FACTS

Agriculture accounts for 20 percent of global greenhouse gas emissions and 70 to 85 percent of water use.

—Sergio Zelaya, the senior land and water officer for the Food and Agriculture Organization of the United Nations livestock to overgraze pastureland, and the application of fossil fuel–based fertilizers and pesticides all release harmful carbon into the atmosphere.

Water: Too Much or Too Little

Farming is also dependent on water, and climate change is threatening this precious commodity as well. Predictable and beneficial cycles of rain are altered by higher temperatures, resulting in fluctuating periods of severe storms and drought. Iowa farmer Justin Jordan has experienced what the future of farming would be like if climate change is not slowed. His farm's 2019 growing season was delayed a month when heavy rains hit, flooding his land and preventing him from planting his corn on time. "I'm looking at a 20-to-30% drop in yield just from the poor spring we had," says Jordan, who was luckier than other area farmers affected by extensive flooding. "I'll be able to plant next year. Some of those guys, those fields are so damaged that they're talking two, three years before they're back in the fields planting again."[31]

The Midwest floods of 2019 struck not only Iowa but also Missouri, Nebraska, South Dakota, and Wisconsin. Triggered by unusually warm spring weather and increased rainfall, rivers, lakes, and reservoirs overflowed, inundating the Plains states and putting some 200 million people at risk of flooding. Rich farmland turned into vast lakes, making future planting uncertain; cattle and pigs drowned, and crops that had already been harvested and stored in silos were ruined. One Iowa farmer estimated that half of his neighbors would not recover from the flood.

Like their American counterparts, East African farmers also experienced floods in 2018 that threatened the food chain that feeds thousands of people. In Kenya, a nation of some 50 million

In 2014, Madan Poudel was a student and agriculture activist from Nepal, one of the world's poorest countries. In a report for the Consultative Group on International Agricultural Research, Poudel described how climate change was impacting his community.

> When I started my Bachelor's level study I became more aware about climate change issues. It became vivid to me that there were lots of changes in Nepal and the agriculture sector, created by a changing climate.
>
> When I ask my grandparents about the timing of cultivating rice, they replied to me that the timing of planting crops is now shifting with onset of rainfall. Whenever I go to the village and have discussions with the villagers about agriculture practices, I feel different scenarios of climate change and its impacts in agriculture.
>
> There is decreasing frequency but increasing intensity of rainfall during summer while delays or complete absence of rain in the winter. The mountainous regions suffer from high exposure of natural disasters such as floods and landslides, erratic rainfall patterns, prolonged drought and hailstorms. . . .
>
> We are seeing how crop production is changing. Oranges are ripening in October, when in previous years, it used to be December. Mustard was successfully sown in late September but now it needs to be planted in early- to mid-September to produce the same yield.
>
> To cope with a changing climate, farmers are beginning to substitute rice crop in khet land (irrigated) with crops that are less water demanding, such as finger millets and wheat.

Madan Poudel, "Climate Change Impacts and Adaptation: Story from My Nepalese Village," Research Program on Climate Change, Agriculture and Food Security, Consultative Group on International Agricultural Research, June 9, 2014. https://ccafs.cgiar.org.

people, rain and floods destroyed farms, swept away livestock, and caused higher food prices due to reduced farm yields and difficulty transporting crops over flooded roads. "Thousands of people have lost their means of livelihood in many parts of Kenya and wider East Africa, which is experiencing heavy rains and increased incidence of flooding,"[32] notes Gabriel Rugalema, who represents the Food and Agriculture Organization of the United Nations in Kenya.

Droughts can be just as damaging to agriculture as floods. Climate change makes wet climates wetter, but it also makes dry climates even drier. Rising temperatures, reduced rainfall, and evaporation of moisture from the ground all combine to further dehydrate areas that already suffer from nutrient-poor, dehydrated soil. This cycle is known as a positive feedback loop: the sun's energy heats the earth, which in turn radiates more heat into the atmosphere, creating a never-ending cycle. As climate change advances, more droughts will occur throughout the world, lasting longer and having a larger impact. "Future intensification of concurrent soil drought and atmospheric aridity," notes Pierre Gentine, an associate professor of earth and environmental engineering, "would be disastrous for ecosystems and greatly impact all aspects of our lives."[33]

Droughts have affected southern Africa, Australia, the Mediterranean, and the United States along the Pacific coast and in the Southwest. Between 2011 and 2017, California experienced one of the worst droughts in its history. Farms growing everything from strawberries and broccoli to walnuts and figs suffered reduced crop yields, resulting in a loss of billions of dollars. Rising temperatures altered the normal rainfall patterns: in 2015 no rain fell for six straight months. Valerie Trouet, an assistant professor at the University of Arizona, notes that "what we are seeing now is fundamentally different from previous mega-droughts, which were driven largely by precipitation. Now, thanks to higher temperatures driven by climate change, droughts are increasingly temperature-driven."[34]

Droughts not only bring with them the hardships of food insecurity, but they also can be a factor in civil unrest and outright conflict. Around the same time as the California drought, Syria suffered a devastating long-term drought that affected some 60 percent of the land and caused enormous hardships for its population. The resulting crop failures and increased food prices forced more than a million Syrians to flee the countryside for the cities. Adding stress to an already volatile situation, the drought was cited as a contributing factor to the Syrian civil war. "We're not saying the drought caused the war," says Columbia University climate scientist Richard Seager. "We're saying that . . . it helped kick things over the threshold into open conflict. And a drought of that severity was made much more likely by the ongoing human-driven drying of that region."[35]

Livestock at Risk

In the global agricultural environment, raising livestock is just as important as growing crops. Cows, pigs, chickens, sheep, and other farm animals produce a host of useful products, including meat, milk, eggs, leather, and wool. They provide transportation in developing countries, generate income for more than 1 billion people worldwide, supply protein for human diets, and fertilize the soil. As the world's standard of living continues to rise, there will be an increased demand for animal products by 2050. But ongoing climate change threatens to disrupt the many benefits provided by livestock.

Livestock, such as cows, get much of their food from pastureland. Droughts reduce the amount of grazing land for livestock, which often forces ranchers to sell off some of their herd.

Many of the necessities that are vital to healthy livestock are adversely affected by rising temperatures. There is, for example, less water for the livestock to consume, and shrinking pastureland means less food for the animals. A hotter environment promotes stress in livestock, leading to more diseases; changes in breeding habits; lower production of meat, milk, and eggs; and a reduction of the animals' body weight. Droughts reduce the amount of grazing land for livestock, forcing ranchers to seek ways to supplement their income. In 2012, Carlyle Currier, a rancher in Molina, Colorado, was forced to decide whether to sell off some of his herd due to a drought-caused decrease in feed crops. "This is probably the worst it's been since 1977," he said. "We just can't grow enough to feed the cattle ourselves." In response to such droughts, some ranchers change their herd's diets to save money, feeding them cheaper but less nutritious grains. "It's like force-feeding cows something they don't really like to eat,"[36] Currier noted. Many ranchers go into debt or take jobs outside of farming to supplement their income in such difficult times.

A Looming Crisis

Less feed for cattle and other livestock means less food on the world's tables. This is a potential disaster, as Earth's population is increasing at an alarming rate. It took from the dawn of time to the year 1800 for the first billion people to populate Earth. In 2019, the world's population increased by about 82 million people; by 2037, an estimated 9 billion will inhabit the planet. All these people will need to be fed, but with climate change shrinking available farmland and reducing crop yield, the world is headed for a crisis of food insecurity, malnutrition, and starvation, especially in the poorer nations. Drought-tolerant crops are becoming more important as global temperatures rise. Researchers are experimenting with genetically modified seeds that are designed to withstand higher temperatures and drought conditions. Farmers have begun to introduce new agricultural techniques as well to increase farm output, but many people fear that their actions may be too little, too late—especially if climate change is not mitigated.

Chapter Four

Climate Change and Health

It has been called the most dangerous creature on the planet. It lives everywhere in the world except Antarctica, Iceland, and a few island nations in the Indian and Pacific Oceans. The female of the species feeds on humans and animals by drinking their blood. Yet it is tiny, measuring only 0.15 to 0.4 inches (3.8 to 20.4 mm). This deadly creature is the lowly mosquito, and for a growing number of people worldwide, it is more than just a nuisance at picnics or a day at the beach. The World Health Organization (WHO) estimates that millions of human deaths each year are caused by mosquitoes, especially as a carrier of the parasite that causes the deadly disease malaria.

Mosquitoes breed most efficiently in areas of high temperature and humidity, which are also the regions whose populations are most vulnerable to the devastating effects of climate change. In these areas, mosquitoes, heat waves, droughts, and changing rainfall patterns impact human well-being and endanger the lives of millions of people. According to Paul R. Epstein, a physician and public health expert who studied the effect of climate change on human health, "The nearly five hundred million people who live in rural areas in dry and semiarid lands—mostly in Asia and Africa but also in parts of Mexico and Brazil—tend to have the lowest levels of health and well-being."[37]

As temperatures rise around the world, the incidence of climate-related health issues is growing. And many of these incidents are tied to the lowliest—but sometimes the most dangerous—of nature's creatures, such as the mosquito.

Vector-Borne Diseases

Earth's warming climate has created an increased risk of spreading infections known as vector-borne diseases. Vector-borne diseases are passed to humans or animals by carriers called vectors, which are not affected by the illnesses they carry. Mosquitoes are a common vector, as are ticks, mites, fleas, and sand flies. A major example of a vector-borne disease is malaria, which is a life-threatening disease that is transmitted to humans by mosquitoes. Malaria's symptoms include headaches, fever, and joint pain, and it can be fatal if not treated in a timely manner. According to WHO, some 3.2 billion people—nearly half the people on Earth—are at risk for contracting malaria; in 2017, more than 435,000 people died of the disease.

As the climate warms, changes in the environment can extend the life span and geographical spread of vectors. One 2019 study estimates that within a century, an additional 1 billion people could become at risk for vector-borne illnesses. Canadian journalist Leslie Young explains how this may occur:

IMPACT FACTS

There are more than three thousand species of mosquitoes in the world, and they spread more diseases than any other creature.

—The National Geographic Society

> Warmer weather means a longer mosquito season . . . and the bugs might be more likely to survive over the winter. Mosquitoes also tend to be more active when it's warm, meaning they're more likely to fly around seeking things to bite. Warm weather means their eggs mature faster, making more mosquitoes. And any diseases they might be carrying also tend to mature more quickly when it's warm out—so are more likely to be transmitted.[38]

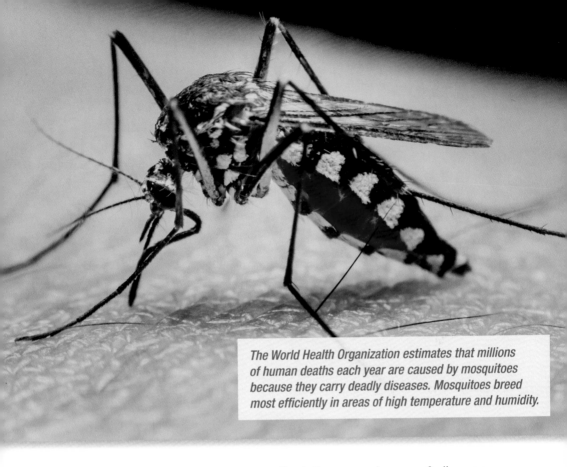

The World Health Organization estimates that millions of human deaths each year are caused by mosquitoes because they carry deadly diseases. Mosquitoes breed most efficiently in areas of high temperature and humidity.

Increased rainfall can also affect the prevalence of disease-carrying mosquitoes. Mosquitoes need water to lay their eggs and to provide an environment for the larvae to mature. In tropical countries, malaria is more prevalent during the rainy season when there are many sources of standing water, such as small puddles, shallow ponds, ditches, and even in hoofprints left by animals. When a region's rainfall cycles are disrupted by climate change, this can raise the frequency of incidents of vector-borne illnesses.

Malaria is not the only disease carried by mosquitoes. West Nile virus, dengue fever, and Zika virus are all transmitted to humans by the bite of a female mosquito. These diseases will be able to find new places to thrive as the world's temperature rises.

The Dangers of Heat

Although warmer weather is beneficial to mosquitoes and other insects, too much heat can be deadly to humans. In 2010, people

The Toxic Air of New Delhi

New Delhi, India, one of the most polluted cities in the world, is often covered by a thick brown haze that obscures the sky. In November 2019, however, the city's air quality reached new levels of danger.

Toxic smog from vehicles, industrial plants, and farmers burning off the remains of harvested crops created such pollution that it could be seen from space. The city declared a public health emergency and limited the number of cars and trucks allowed to drive the city's streets. Even for healthy citizens of New Delhi, stepping out of their houses poses risks. "I have patients from all age groups," says throat specialist Salil Sharma, "and most of them are non-smokers who complain of breathlessness, chest congestion, fatigue and weakness. In some cases, I had to put some patients on a ventilator because they couldn't breathe. We are right in the middle of a health emergency."

In 2017, air pollution claimed 12.4 million lives in India. It was a wake-up call that the country took to heart. In 2019, officials announced the National Clean Air Program, a five-year plan to clean up India's most polluted cities by setting targets for the reduction of smog and improving air-quality monitoring.

Quoted in Doyle Rice, "New Delhi's Toxic, Polluted Air Chokes City's 20 Million People, and the Haze Can Be Seen from Space," *USA Today*, November 5, 2019. www.usatoday.com.

were suffering through a scorching summer heat wave of unrelenting high temperatures and humidity that affected much of the world, including the United States. Logan, a young high school football player in Arkansas, fell ill during a practice session, complaining of weakness and fatigue. By the time he sought treatment, he had developed heatstroke and kidney failure. It took kidney dialysis to ultimately save Logan's life. Around the country, and especially in the Southeast, stories of heat-induced illness are becoming more common. But unlike Logan, some victims succumb to the risks of participating in high school football in hot weather. "Heat is already a major safety hazard for athletes and the broader public," says Andrew Grundstein, a professor of climate science at the University of Georgia. "Yet we should still be able to do the activities like sports that we enjoy. Considering that our climate is warming, it is even more important that we have heat safety guidelines and policies. This will help us adapt and be more prepared for the more frequent hot conditions."[39]

Although temperature variations are a normal part of the worldwide climate cycle, days or weeks of high temperatures combined with humidity can seriously affect populations. Urban areas are particularly vulnerable to heat waves caused by a phenomenon known as the heat island effect. This is due to the fact that buildings and asphalt or concrete streets retain more heat than surrounding suburban and rural areas. In essence, city environments heat up and stay hot for longer periods, worsening incidents of heatstroke and other heat-related illnesses for urban populations. In the United States, Albuquerque, Denver, and Las Vegas are the cities with the greatest temperature differences between their urban and rural areas. In 2005, Las Vegas experienced a deadly heat wave in which more than fifteen people died as the temperature reached a record 117°F (47°C).

Heat waves are on the rise. During the 1960s, urban areas across the United States experienced about two heat waves every year; by the 2010s, that number had increased to six annually. Shubhayu Saha, a health scientist with the Climate and Health Program at the Centers for Disease Control and Prevention, notes that studies confirm the risks of increasing heat waves. "The projections are that the number of deaths and illness will increase in the years to come as the summers become longer and the heat becomes more intense,"[40] Saha says.

Climate Change and Respiratory Health

There are many chronic illnesses that are made worse by heat and hot environments. Respiratory disorders, for example, impact about 1 billion people globally, and these include asthma, allergies, pneumonia, lung cancer, and tuberculosis. According to WHO, chronic obstructive pulmonary disease is one of the deadliest of these diseases, killing 3 million people annually—the third leading cause of death worldwide. Asthma affects about

334 million people worldwide and is the most common chronic disease among children.

Although these statistics are disturbing, climate change is making them more devastating. Polluted air contributes to numerous diseases involving the lungs and the cardiovascular system, causing 4.2 million deaths in 2016 alone. A recent study revealed that one out of every nine deaths worldwide is caused by air pollution. According to physician Maria Neira of WHO, "Few risks have a greater impact on global health today than air pollution."[41] And one of the major culprits of this problem is the greenhouse gas ozone.

Ozone in the upper atmosphere adds to the heat-trapping role of greenhouse gases. But down near the surface of the earth, it is ground-level ozone that presents a very real risk to human health. When sunlight reacts with emissions from cars, trucks, and factories, it causes a harmful pollution called smog, of which ozone is a major component. As greenhouse gases in the atmo-

Experts say that with a warming climate it is important that athletic programs, such as high school football, develop heat safety guidelines and policies.

sphere raise temperatures, the concentration of ozone at ground level also increases. People who already have a respiratory disease are most vulnerable to the effects of this pollution. A 2011 report by the Union of Concerned Scientists says that by 2050, 11.8 million more cases of worsening respiratory symptoms (such as wheezing, coughing, and shortness of breath) could occur if climate change continues. Thousands of additional hospitalizations are likely to occur, especially among infants and the elderly.

Polluted Water

Just as polluted air can circulate disease, contaminated water also promotes the spread of various illnesses that endanger the health of a large share of the world's population. Although water covers most of the globe, only a minuscule portion, about 3 percent, is freshwater suitable for human consumption. With climate change affecting the amount and intensity of rainfall, and thus the danger of more flooding, the chances of increased contamination of this essential resource from polluted runoff are growing.

IMPACT FACTS

As many as half of all rivers in Asia are contaminated with bacteria, viruses, and other organic pathogens.

—United Nations Environment Programme

About 1.3 billion people around the world live in areas that put them at risk for contracting cholera, a disease that is transmitted to humans by a bacterium found in contaminated water. People who contract cholera suffer from vomiting, diarrhea, cramps, and rapid heart rate. If left untreated, cholera can cause death by dehydration in mere hours; more than 140,000 people succumb to the disease each year. Cholera occurs most frequently in developing countries where clean water is scarce and sanitation is poor. In Algeria, Bangladesh, Haiti, Somalia, and other developing countries, water containing the cholera bacterium often contaminates the local drinking supply—and climate change makes it easier for the disease to spread.

Cholera thrives in warmer water, so as the oceans retain more heat, they produce an aquatic environment conducive to the cholera bacterium. According to Mohammad Ali, a senior scientist at the International Vaccine Institute in South Korea, "When temperature goes up by 1 degree Celsius, there is a chance of cholera cases doubling in four months' time and if rainfall goes up by 200 millimeters, then in two months' time, cholera cases will go up by 1.6 folds."[42] Besides cholera, the spread of other waterborne diseases, such as typhoid fever, dysentery, giardia, and others, can increase due to climate change.

Other contaminants can also pollute water and lead to harmful consequences. Flooding from Hurricane Katrina not only caused massive property damage and loss of life but also dumped raw sewage, pesticides, oil, and toxic industrial chemicals into the New Orleans groundwater supply. The health and ecological damage caused by Katrina will have long-term impacts on the region. "The range of toxic chemicals that may have been released is extensive," says professor Lynn Goldman of Johns Hopkins University. "We're talking about metals, persistent chemicals, solvents, [and] materials that have numerous potential health impacts over the long term."[43] Katrina is a warning of things to come as climate change creates larger and more deadly hurricanes.

IMPACT FACTS

Climate change is expected to account for some 250,000 additional deaths every year between 2030 and 2050.

—World Health Organization

The Hidden Effects of Climate Change

The physical impact of increased illnesses due to climate change are easily observed. The wheezing of asthma sufferers, the heatstroke victims during a heat wave, and the vomiting and diarrhea of people who have contracted cholera are all visible signs of maladies that will become more widespread as Earth warms. Although most research centers on the physical aspects

An aerial shot shows flooding in Houston, Texas, from Hurricane Harvey in 2017. Flooding from intense and increasing rainfall can cause polluted run-off water to mix with and contaminate drinking water supplies.

of climate change, there are other effects that are more subtle but just as debilitating. These are the psychological impacts of a changing environment.

"People have been concerned and distressed about climate change for several decades," notes Joseph Reser, a psychologist at Griffith University in Australia. "Climate change is an ongoing threat, and the psychological implications are occurring here and now."[44] A 2018 study by the Yale Program on Climate Change Communication found that 62 percent of adult Americans were worried about climate change. This anxiety stems from the fear of increasing natural disasters attributed to climate change, such as more severe hurricanes, deadlier heat waves, and worsening droughts and floods.

For people who have been through a traumatic disaster, such as Hurricane Dorian, the experience takes a toll on their mental health. "A lot of them are confused," says the Reverend Elvis Burrows, who helped victims in the aftermath of Dorian. "Some

Chicago is a city known for its extreme temperatures, from teeth-chattering winters to sweltering summers. But even this world-class city was unprepared for the deadly heat wave of 1995.

It was one of the worst urban heat waves in US history, with the temperature soaring to a scorching 106°F (41°C) in July 1995, generating a heat index of 125°F (52°C). Chicagoans coped with the intense heat as best they could, thronging to public swimming pools and air-conditioned buildings. Cubs fans who attended baseball games at Wrigley Field tried to keep cool with wet towels on their heads. But it was the poor and elderly living in crowded apartments with no air-conditioning who suffered the most. Many of these Chicagoans stayed home with closed windows overnight for reasons of personal safety.

The city was unprepared for the severity of the heat wave. Emergency rooms were overcrowded with patients suffering from heatstroke, and all of Chicago's fifty-six ambulances and six hundred paramedics were overwhelmed by the nearly constant emergency calls. By the time the heat wave ended three days later, 739 people had perished.

The 1995 heat wave led Chicago to improve its emergency response system. When another one struck four years later, the city was ready with emergency press releases, free transportation to cooling centers, and house-to-house police wellness checks on elderly residents. This time, the death toll was 110—still tragic, but an indication of lessons learned.

of them had to spend entire nights in ceilings [to escape rising water or] on jet skis trying to get out from their homes. Some of them had to just ride it out in extremely dangerous situations. And they're traumatized."[45] Depression, anxiety, stress, insomnia, and feelings of insecurity are some of the mental effects disasters can have on people. There are also more serious effects, such as post-traumatic stress disorder, and suicidal thoughts or even suicide attempts, which can plague survivors of a disaster long after the event has passed.

Community health is another aspect of the impact of climate change. According to a report by the American Psychological Association and the environmental marketing group ecoAmerica, "Individual well-being is supported not only by a healthy mind in a healthy body, but by a healthy community and a healthy network of social relationships."[46] Disasters can break down these relationships, leading to increased domestic violence and criminal activity, a less unified community, diminished feelings of belonging, and other types of social conflict. In 2017, a study was conducted to learn the effects of climate change on the indigenous Inuit community living in Rigolet, a small town in northern Canada. Warming waters and melting sea ice are affecting their lives and livelihoods, forcing the Inuit to alter a lifestyle that goes back for generations. Interviews with some one hundred residents revealed stress, anxiety, and even grief brought on by the changes. "People talked about feeling depressed and feeling trapped in the community. Feeling unable to get out," says Ashlee Cunsolo, a researcher who took part in the study. "One person described it like feeling like a caged animal. The conditions weren't allowing for those regular trips out on the ice or into the environment."[47]

"It's our identity as Inuit people," says Derrick Pottle of the land around Rigolet. "It's our connection to who we are."[48] That connection is being altered by climate change, and many people worldwide, along with the Inuit people, are feeling the mental and physical health effects of a hotter, more inhospitable world.

Chapter Five

Climate Change Solutions

On September 20, 2019, thirteen-year-old Anna Siegel of Yarmouth, Maine, skipped school. So did Evan Meneses, seventeen, of Adelaide, Australia, and twelve-year-old Yola Mgogwana of Cape Town, South Africa. These students were doing something more important than just playing hooky. They were participating in the global climate strike along with other students (and many adults) who put off their regular school and job responsibilities to raise awareness of the dangers of climate change.

Demonstrators in some 150 countries around the world took part in the strike. In New York City, four hundred thousand protesters thronged the streets of Manhattan in the largest climate-related demonstration ever held. And although many of the student protesters could not yet vote, their message to their governments was clear. "I want to change the world," stated Baily Carr, a fifteen-year-old who participated in the climate strike, "and I think everyone else in this movement does too."[49]

Changing the world, however, is not an easy task. Although two plans for dealing with climate change were created during the late 1990s and early 2000s, they turned out to be less than successful.

Early International Agreements

In December 1997, a conference was held in Kyoto, Japan, to discuss ways to fight climate change. The result was the Kyoto Protocol, an international agreement that set goals for the reduction of greenhouse gases. The Kyoto Protocol set a 2012 deadline for nations to reduce their emissions of greenhouse gases to below 1990 levels. But many nations, including the heavy polluters China and India, were exempted from the agreement. In 2001, President George W. Bush withdrew the United States from the treaty, claiming that it would hurt the US economy. By the time the deadline arrived, most of the participating countries had not met their emission reduction goals, and the levels of greenhouse gases in the atmosphere continued to rise.

A new treaty intended to replace the Kyoto Protocol was adopted in Paris, France, on December 12, 2015. The Paris Agreement set the goal of limiting the rise in world temperature to no more than 1.5°C (2.7°F) by the year 2100. But the agreement has encountered some setbacks. Most nations are well behind in progress toward their goals. In 2017, President Donald Trump announced his intention to withdraw the United States from the Paris Agreement, potentially motivating other countries to abandon the treaty as well. Of thirty-two countries that account for some 80 percent of all greenhouse gas emissions, few have made efforts toward reducing greenhouse gases.

It is far from certain that the Paris Agreement will be enough to turn the tide of a warming Earth. But despite its problems, progress is being made in the fight against climate change.

Carbon Mitigation

Sweden is a prime example of successful mitigation—that is, the reduction of atmospheric carbon emissions. According to Joshua S. Goldstein and Staffan A. Qvist, the authors of *A Bright Future*, "Sweden became the most successful country in history at expanding low-carbon electricity generation, and leading the way

How Teens Feel About Climate Change

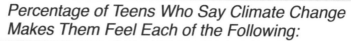

Most US teens view climate change as an important issue, according to a 2019 Kaiser Family Foundation/Washington Post survey that included a sample of US teens between the ages of thirteen and seventeen. When asked how the issue of climate change makes them feel, the predominant feelings described by teens are fear, motivation, and anger. A smaller percentage of teen respondents describe themselves as optimistic.

Percentage of Teens Who Say Climate Change Makes Them Feel Each of the Following:

Feeling	Percentage
Afraid	57%
Motivated	54%
Angry	52%
Helpless	43%
Guilty	42%
Optimistic	29%
Uninterested	20%

Source: Liz Hamel et al, "The Kaiser Family Foundation/Washington Post Climate Change Survey," Washington Post/Kaiser Family Foundation Survey Project, November 27, 2019. www.kff.org.

on climate change."[50] Sweden's carbon mitigation program began in the 1970s, when the country's leaders were looking for new power sources to accommodate a growing demand for electricity. After rejecting fossil fuels as an unacceptable source, the Swedes turned to a different form of power called *kärnkraft*. This fuel is inexpensive, reliable, efficient, and emits no greenhouse gases. *Kärnkraft* is the Swedish word for "nuclear power," and as of 2019, the nation had three nuclear power plants operating eight nuclear reactors. These facilities produce about 40 percent of the nation's electricity. The use of *kärnkraft*, along with other clean sources of energy, has helped Sweden virtually eliminate fossil fuels as a power source for electricity production.

Other countries are also replacing fossil fuels with nuclear power. France's fifty-eight nuclear reactors generate almost 75 percent of the country's electric power, making it the world's top user of nuclear energy for providing electricity. The United States, by comparison, generates only about 20 percent of its electricity from nuclear power plants. China, with forty-six nuclear reactors operating in 2019, is building eleven more to accommodate the demand for electric power by a growing population. The nation is also developing new nuclear technology, including a high-temperature, gas-cooled reactor and a small modular reactor suitable for use in remote areas.

IMPACT FACTS

In 2019, the concentration of carbon dioxide in the atmosphere was 412 parts per million, the highest in 650,000 years.

—NASA

Agriculture can also play an important part in mitigation, and many technologies are available to help farmers counter climate change. No-till farming, for example, is the process of planting crops without tilling, or turning the soil over. This farming method helps soil retain more of the moisture and organic matter that produce healthier crops, and it also helps prevent soil erosion. Likewise, because it does not require tractors or other farming equipment to till fields, it reduces fossil fuel use.

Renewable Energy Sources

Along with carbon mitigation, renewable energy—energy that is continually being replenished, such as wind, solar, and hydropower—is becoming an important part of the fight against climate change. Renewable energy is also called clean energy because it creates no greenhouse gases or other pollutants. Renewable energy infrastructure can be as vast as thousands of wind turbines generating electricity for an urban power grid or as small as a few solar panels providing electricity to a single home. Renewable energy not only helps to save the planet, but it saves money as well. According to the World Economic Forum, in 2016 using wind and solar power became cheaper than using fossil fuels.

Around the world, businesses and individuals are investing in these renewable energy sources. The United States has some of the world's largest wind farms. Major companies, including General Motors, Google, and Walmart, have set a goal to switch to 100 percent renewable power sources, many relying on wind power. Google has reached that goal, with wind power providing 95 percent of its electricity. Solar power is also becoming more prevalent in the United States. About 2 million US homes generate their own electricity through rooftop solar panels. Other solar technologies have also joined the mix. For example, some homeowners are installing ground-level solar panels with automatic sun trackers. The trackers move the panels to make the best use of sunlight in a particular area, thus maximizing the electrical output. In Sweden, the development of *kärnkraft* has allowed the nation to move away from power sources that produce greenhouse gases. But even with this successful conversion, Sweden is still moving toward renewable power. It has set an ambitious goal of generating 100 percent of its electricity needs from renewables by 2040. In 2019, about 11 percent of Sweden's electricity was generated by wind power via some thirty-six hundred wind turbines, and that number is growing.

Norway, Sweden's neighbor to the west, has abundant water resources, and is one of the world's largest users of hydropower. This renewable source, which harnesses the energy in rivers and coastal tides, generates 99 percent of the nation's electricity needs.

IMPACT FACTS

Wind power in the United States has the capacity to generate 96,433 megawatts of electricity, enough to power 25 million homes.

—US Department of Energy

Solar power is becoming more prevalent in the United States. About 2 million US homes generate their own electricity through rooftop solar panels.

China, the world's largest user of coal-fired power plants, is investing in wind and solar power to counteract that country's serious air pollution problem. In the city of Jinan, a new solar road is being tested. Instead of standard concrete, 1.2 miles (2 km) of the Jinan Expressway are paved with transparent concrete. Beneath this surface is a layer of solar cells that generate enough electricity to power eight hundred homes. Besides producing clean energy, future solar roadways could power their own lights, signs, and traffic signals and include heating elements for snow-free driving. As self-driving cars become more established, they also could interact with the solar roadway, making driving safer.

IMPACT FACTS

The sun continually provides Earth with 173,000 terawatts of energy, more than ten thousand times the world's total energy use.

—US Department of Energy

Greta Thunberg might look like a typical teenage girl, but looks can be deceiving. The sixteen-year-old from Sweden is the vanguard of a new generation of climate change activists, and she is not shy about voicing her opinion.

Born in Stockholm in 2003, Thunberg began caring about the climate when she was eight years old. She adopted a low-carbon lifestyle by avoiding air travel and becoming a vegan. At fifteen, Thunberg skipped school and instead sat in front of the Swedish parliament every day for three weeks to protest her government's inaction on climate change. She called her protest a school strike, and it led to school strikes for climate change around the world.

In August 2019, Thunberg came to New York (traveling by sailboat, not airplane) to attend the UN Climate Action Summit. At the conference, she chastised world leaders for not working harder against climate change: "This is all wrong. I shouldn't be up here. I should be back in school on the other side of the ocean. Yet you all come to us young people for hope. How dare you. You have stolen my dreams and my childhood with your empty words."

Thunberg's outspoken passion has brought her many accolades throughout the world. *Time* magazine selected her as the magazine's 2019 Person of the Year, praising her creation of a worldwide movement that promises to become a major force in the fight against climate change.

Quoted in NPR Staff, "Transcript: Greta Thunberg's Speech at the UN Climate Action Summit," NPR, September 23, 2019. www.npr.org.

Sequestering Carbon

Along with reducing levels of greenhouse gases in the atmosphere through mitigation and renewable energy, nations are looking at holding those gases in carbon sinks so they do not enter the atmosphere. Forests are natural carbon sinks, and efforts to restore forests ravaged by excessive logging will help keep harmful gases out of the atmosphere. Thomas Crowther, a professor of environmental systems science, says reforestation is "so much more vastly powerful than anyone ever expected. By far, it's the top climate change solution in terms of carbon storage potential."[51]

Many nations have already committed to reforestation. The African Forest Landscape Restoration Initiative is planning to restore 247 million acres (100 million ha) of land in Africa by 2030. In 2014, Pakistan created the Billion Tree Tsunami, a program to plant 100 billion trees to revitalize the nation's forests. Pakistan reached its goal in 2017, months ahead of schedule. "The project is naturally restoring a previously deforested landscape," says project director Muhammad Tehmasip, "and offers multiple benefits for climate adaptation and mitigation in a very climate-vulnerable province."[52]

Another method of storing carbon is geologic sequestration, in which emissions from factories and power plants are captured and stored in underground geologic formations such as porous rock or depleted gas and oil reservoirs. Many companies are developing the technology for capturing carbon emissions, and the US Geological Survey has identified thirty-six regions around the country that have underground geological features suitable for carbon storage.

Decatur, Illinois, is the site of an ambitious project, begun in 2017, to store carbon dioxide gas underground. Called the Illinois Industrial Carbon Capture Project, its technology removes carbon dioxide from the exhaust of an ethanol production plant owned by agricultural giant Archer Daniels Midland (ADM). The gas is then compressed and sent through pipes to soft sandstone deposits about 1.5 miles (2.4 km) underground. The project's goal is to store 1.1 million tons (998 t) of carbon dioxide annually for five years. "The technology that we are using in Decatur," says Todd Werpy, ADM's chief technology officer, "can be a model for reducing industrial carbon emissions around the world."[53]

One of the newest technologies for capturing carbon dioxide from the atmosphere has been invented by Klaus Lackner, the director of the Center for Negative Carbon Emissions at Arizona State University. Lackner developed a device sometimes referred to as a "mechanical tree" that absorbs atmospheric carbon dioxide just as trees do. But it does the job thousands of times more efficiently than a real tree. The device uses panels of absorbent material that are extended into the air to collect carbon dioxide and trap it for sequestering or sale to industry for various uses. "Carbon dioxide is a waste product we produce every time we drive our cars or turn on the lights in our homes, "says Lackner. "Our device can recycle it, bringing it out of the atmosphere [to] either bury it or use it as an industrial gas."[54]

Adapting to Climate Change

Although efforts are under way to lessen the severity of climate change by reducing greenhouse gas emissions, many observers recognize that humanity will have to adapt to the changes already taking place. Climate change is forcing many people to alter their way of life, as increasing temperatures affect agriculture and rising seas threaten coastal habitations. This is especially evident in poorer regions, where people have neither the technology nor the scientific knowledge to mitigate climate change.

Kiribati, for example, is a nation composed of thirty-three atolls and reef islands in the central Pacific Ocean. Rising sea levels have put Kiribati in a perilous position: if climate change continues, the nation could be underwater by 2100. Already two of the nation's islands have been overtaken by rising water. "Kiribati is vulnerable to climate change and sea level rise which we can see the effects of visually," says Tebutonga Ereata of Kiribati's Ministry of Environment, Lands and Agriculture Development. "There are places that have been eroded quite seriously. We are already vulnerable now."[55] The entire village of Tebontebike has had to move inland as the rising sea claimed more land; residents fear that they will soon have to move again.

Kiribati created a plan for its people should the unthinkable occur. In 2014, the nation purchased 7.7 square miles (20 km²) of land in the Fiji islands as a refuge for the population should their homeland be completely inundated. In 2016, however, the new government in Kiribati put this plan on hold, and politicians continue to debate whether the population should migrate or stay in Kiribati to fight climate change.

In the meantime, the Kiribati Adaptation Program works to reduce the nation's vulnerability to the effects of climate change. The program has constructed seawalls to prevent seawater incursion, and it has increased the planting of mangroves, which are small trees that grow well in coastal areas and salt marshes. Mangrove trees help reduce shoreline erosion and act as natural sea walls to protect the coastline from wind and waves.

Such adaptations can help countries lessen the impacts of climate change. Another helpful adaptation involves the development of new farming practices to counteract the damage that rising temperatures and stronger winds have on farmland. In Bangladesh, where rising sea levels have increased the salt content of cropland, farmers are turning to fishing and shrimp farming to replace crops that cannot grow in the salt-laden soil. In Costa Rica, coffee has been a major crop since the 1800s, but climate change is making coffee harder to grow. Many farmers, faced

Kiribati (pictured) is a nation of thirty-three islands in the central Pacific Ocean. If climate change and rising seas levels continue, Kiribati could be underwater by 2100.

Carbon Footprints

Everyone has a carbon footprint. Unlike a physical footprint, it cannot be seen, but it has a real impact on Earth's climate. A carbon footprint is the amount of greenhouse gases released as a result of the everyday activities of humans, whether individually, as a group, or even as a nation. A simple shopping trip, for example, adds to a carbon footprint through the use of the fossil fuel that powers the car to get there. At the store, heating, air-conditioning, and lighting all run on power that may have been generated by power plants that produce greenhouse gases. Likewise, the manufacturing and transportation of the goods for sale likely adds more carbon to the atmosphere.

Carbon footprints can be reduced in several ways. Driving a fuel-efficient gasoline or electric car can cut the amount of vehicle exhaust emitted. Better insulation and more efficient appliances can lower a home's footprint. Utility companies can convert to clean energy such as wind and hydropower to lower their carbon emissions. Businesses can replace distant meetings and conferences with videoconferences, thereby avoiding the need to fly participants to meetings and thus reducing their carbon footprint. Even eating less meat can reduce carbon emissions because growing vegetables creates less carbon than raising livestock.

with losing their livelihoods, have turned to growing oranges as an alternative to coffee. In the town of Hojancha, for example, orange trees have been found to be more resistant to the impact of climate change.

As a global problem, climate change can only be conquered if the nations of the world come together to find solutions that, ultimately, will benefit all humankind. The students who went on strike in the fall of 2019—protesting government inaction in confronting climate change—are the future not only of their home countries but also of the world. Their movement had an auspicious beginning as the young environmentalists thronged the streets of New York, New Delhi, and other cities worldwide. They raised their voices in protest, hoping that those in power would finally listen.

Piers Forster, a professor of climate physics at the University of Leeds in the United Kingdom, also conveyed the need for international cooperation in eliminating climate change: "You have to get every country in the world to do it, and you have to get every part of the economy interested. So that's where the challenge is, but I would say that humanity always rises to these challenges, so I'm personally quite optimistic."[56]

Forster's optimism is strong despite obstacles that have slowed the search for a solution to the climate change problem. But not everyone shares his outlook. Time is running out, and climate change is speeding up, driving the world toward a new climatic era. The question is, can people slow climate change before it is too late? The answer is still unclear.

Introduction: A Deadly Heat Wave

1. Quoted in Isabelle Gerretsen and Brandon Miller, "Record Heat Waves Might Have Made July the Hottest Month Ever Recorded," CNN, August 1, 2019. www.cnn.com.

2. Quoted in Umair Irfan, "108 Degrees in Paris: Europe is Shattering Heat Records This Week," Vox, July 20, 2019. www.vox.com.

3. Quoted in Drew Kahn, "Landmark UN Report Warns Sea Levels Will Rise Faster than Projected by 2100," CNN, September 25, 2019. www.cnn.com.

Chapter One: Climate Change and Natural Disasters

4. Quoted in Kendra Pierre-Louis, "Why Does California Have So Many Wildfires?," *New York Times*, November 9, 2018. www.nytimes.com.

5. Steve Nix, "When and Where Do Wildfires Occur?," ThoughtCo, May 4, 2018. www.thoughtco.com.

6. Climate Central, *Global Weirdness: Severe Storms, Deadly Heat Waves, Relentless Drought, Rising Seas, and the Weather of the Future*. New York: Pantheon, 2012, p. 116.

7. Quoted in Sara Peach, "Sea Surface Temperatures Drive Hurricane Strength," Yale Climate Connections, August 3, 2016. www.yaleclimateconnections.org.

8. Quoted in Sanya Mansoor, "Hurricane Dorian Is Barely Moving at All. Here's Why That Makes It Especially Dangerous," *Time*, September 3, 2019. www.time.com.

9. Quoted in Joanna Walters, "Hurricane Dorian: Slow-Moving Storm Batters Bahamas," *The Guardian*, September 3, 2019. www.theguardian.com.

10. Quoted in Geophysical Fluid Dynamics Laboratory, "Global Warming and Hurricanes: An Overview of Current Research Results," August 15, 2019. www.gfdl.noaa.gov.

11. Third National Climate Assessment, "Global Climate Change Impacts in the United States," US Global Change Research Program, 2014. https://nca2014.globalchange.gov.

12. Quoted in Jeff Tollefson, "Global Warming Already Driving Increases in Rainfall Extremes," *Nature*, March 7, 2016. www.nature.com.

13. Quoted in K.A. Shaji, "As Floods Repeat This Year in Kerala, Experts Point to Climate Change," Mongabay, August 13, 2019. https://india.mongabay.com.

14. Union of Concerned Scientists, "Causes of Drought: What's the Climate Connection?" www.ucsusa.org.

15. Quoted in Anne M. Stark, "Human Impact on Droughts Goes Back 100 Years," Lawrence Livermore National Laboratory, May 1, 2019. www.llnl.gov.

16. Quoted in Alan Collins, "Drought Impact on Shelby County Farmers," WBRC, September 6, 2019. www.wbrc.com.

17. Doyle Rice, "'Breaking' the Heat Index: US Heat Waves to Skyrocket as Globe Warms, Study Suggests," *USA Today*, July 16, 2019. www.usatoday.com.

Chapter Two: Climate Change and the Oceans

18. Quoted in Daisy Hernandez, "Climate Change Has Claimed Its First Icelandic Glacier," *Popular Mechanics*, July 22, 2019. www.popularmechanics.com.

19. James Hansen et al., "Ice Melt, Sea Level Rise and Superstorms: Evidence from Paleoclimate Data, Climate Modeling, and Modern Observations That 2°C Global Warming Could Be Dangerous," *Atmospheric Chemistry and Physics*, March 22, 2016, p. 3762.

20. Quoted in Leanna Garfield, "Sea-Level Rise Is a Huge, Overlooked Economic Threat to New York City, According to the Official in Charge of Keeping the City from Flooding," *Business Insider*, August 22, 2017. www.businessinsider.com.

21. Quoted in Eleanor Ainge Roy, "'One Day We'll Disappear': Tuvalu's Sinking Islands," *The Guardian*, May 16, 2019. www.theguardian.com.

22. Quoted in Roy, "'One Day We'll Disappear.'"

23. Henry Wismayer, "A Future Without Long-Haul Vacations," *The Atlantic*, September 2, 2019. www.theatlantic.com.

24. Quoted in Todd Hollingshead, "Melting Ice Is Forcing Polar Bears to Swim More; the Cost Is High," BYU News, January 30, 2018. https://news.byu.edu.

25. Quoted in Cleve R. Wootson Jr., "Polar Bears Hurt by Climate Change Are More Likely to Turn to a New Food Source—Humans," *Washington Post*, July 13, 2017. www.washington post.com.

26. Quoted in Woods Hole Oceanographic Institution, "Study Finds Emperor Penguin in Peril," June 29, 2014. www.whoi .edu.

Chapter Three: Climate Change and Agriculture

27. IPCC, "2019: Summary for Policymakers," in *Climate Change and Land: An IPCC Special Report on Climate Change, Desertification, Land Degradation, Sustainable Land Management, Food Security, and Greenhouse Gas Fluxes in Terrestrial Ecosystems,* ed. P.R. Shukla et al., August 7, 2019. https://www.ipcc.ch.

28. Quoted in Amanda Little, *The Fate of Food: What We'll Eat in a Bigger, Hotter, Smarter World.* New York: Harmony, 2019, p. 7.

29. Quoted in Georgina Gustin, "Climate Change Could Lead to Major Crop Failures in World's Biggest Corn Regions," Inside-Climate News, June 11, 2018. www.insideclimatenews.org.

30. Quoted in Joseph Romm, *Climate Change: What Everyone Needs to Know*. New York: Oxford University Press, 2018, p. 130.

31. Quoted in Bill Weir, "Scientists Say Farmers Could Grow Their Way Out of the Climate Crisis," CNN, August 8, 2019. www .cnn.com.

32. Quoted in *EastAfrican,* "Hunger Looms as Floods Destroy Crops, Sweep Away Animals in East Africa," May 12, 2018. www.theeastafrican.co.ke.

33. Quoted in ScienceDaily, "New Feedback Phenomenon Found to Drive Increasing Drought and Aridity," September 2, 2019. www.sciencedaily.com.

34. Quoted in Climate Signals, "California Drought 2011–2016," December 4, 2018. www.climatesignals.org.

35. Quoted in Mark Fischetti, "Climate Change Hastened Syria's Civil War," *Scientific American,* March 2, 2015. www.scientific american.com.

36. Quoted in Susan Moran, "U.S. Ranchers Struggle to Adapt to Climate Change," *Scientific American,* November 14, 2012. www.scientificamerican.com.

Chapter Four: Climate Change and Health

37. Paul R. Epstein and Dan Ferber, *Changing Planet, Changing Health: How the Climate Crisis Threatens Our Health and What We Can Do About It.* Berkeley: University of California Press, 2011, p. 118.

38. Leslie Young, "Mosquitoes Are on the Move Due to Climate Change, and They Could Bring Diseases," Global News, August 25, 2019. www.globalnews.ca.

39. Quoted in James Bruggers, "'This Was Preventable': Football Heat Deaths and the Rising Temperature," InsideClimate News, July 20, 2018. www.insideclimatenews.org.

40. Quoted in Jaclyn Jeffrey-Wilensky, "Without Swift Action on Climate Change, Heat Waves Could Kill Thousands in U.S. Cities," NBC News Mach, June 16, 2019. www.nbcnews .com.

41. Quoted in World Health Organization, "7 Million Premature Deaths Annually Linked to Air Pollution," news release, March 25, 2014. www.who.int.

42. Quoted in Tan Ee Lyn, "Cholera Outbreaks Closely Follow Temperature Rise, Rainfall," Reuters, May 31, 2011. www .reuters.com.

43. Quoted in Larry West, "The Environmental Impacts of Hurricane Katrina," ThoughtCo, May 8, 2019. www.thoughtco .com.

44. Quoted in Kirsten Weir, "Climate Change Is Threatening Mental Health," American Psychological Society, *Monitor on Psychology*, July/August 2016. www.apa.org.

45. Quoted in Brooke Shafer and Michael Mora, "After Hurricane Dorian, an Emphasis on Mental Health in the Bahamas," WINK News, September 12, 2019. www.winknews.com.
46. Susan Clayton, Christie Manning, and Caroline Hodge, *Beyond Storms & Droughts: The Psychological Impacts of Climate Change*. Washington, DC: American Psychological Association and ecoAmerica, 2014.
47. Quoted in Sabrina Fabian, "Trapped 'Like a Caged Animal': Climate Change Taking Toll on Mental Health of Inuit," CBC News, May 27, 2017. www.cbc.ca.
48. Quoted in Fabian, "Trapped 'Like a Caged Animal.'"

Chapter Five: Climate Change Solutions
49. Quoted in Kashmira Gander, "'Our Futures Are at Risk': Meet the Kids Skipping School to Join the Global Climate Strike," *Newsweek*, September 17, 2019. www.newsweek.com.
50. Joshua S. Goldstein and Staffan A. Qvist, *A Bright Future: How Some Countries Have Solved Climate Change and the Rest Can Follow*. New York: Public Affairs, 2019, p. 27.
51. Quoted in Umair Irfan, "Restoring Forests May Be One of Our Most Powerful Weapons in Fighting Climate Change," Vox, July 5, 2019. www.vox.com.
52. Quoted in International Union for Conservation of Nature, "Pakistan's Billion Tree Tsunami Restores 350,000 Hectares of Forests and Degraded Land to Surpass Bonn Challenge Commitment," August 11, 2017. www.iucn.org.
53. Quoted in Chris Mooney, "The Quest to Capture and Store Carbon—and Slow Climate Change—Just Reached a New Milestone," *Washington Post,* April 10, 2017. www.washingtonpost.com.
54. Quoted in Skip Derra, "Lackner's Carbon-Capture Technology Moves to Commercialization," ASU Now, April 29, 2019. www.asunow.asu.edu.
55. Quoted in Republic of Kiribati, "Climate Change," August 10, 2010. www.climate.gov.ki.
56. Quoted in Jasmine Aguilera, "Is This Summer's Intense Heat Caused by Climate Change?," *Time*, August 5, 2019, p. 10.

1. Unplug laptops, phone chargers, and other electronics when not in use; they can use electricity ("vampire power") even when turned off.

2. Walking or biking instead of driving will help reduce your carbon footprint.

3. Help reduce ocean pollution by using reusable bottles, straws, and utensils rather than plastic ones.

4. In winter, wear a sweater or hoodie around the house instead of raising the thermostat.

5. When you leave a room, turn off the lights.

6. Eating less beef (or replacing it with chicken) helps lower the greenhouse gases emitted by livestock production.

7. On trips to the ocean, rivers, and lakes, picking up trash (yours or someone else's) will help keep garbage out of waterways.

8. Eat locally produced food whenever possible; it reduces the carbon emitted by delivery vehicles.

9. When craving fast food, go into the restaurant instead of letting your car idle in the drive-through lane.

10. Recycle whatever you can, and consider shopping at thrift stores for fashionable used clothing.

11. Consider joining (or organizing) a climate strike to raise awareness of the dangers of climate change.

12. Study climate science in school or on your own, and consider a career helping to solve the problem of climate change.

Climate.gov—www.climate.gov

This site is part of the National Oceanic and Atmospheric Administration, whose mission is to keep the public informed about the changing environment. Its website examines the issue of climate change by providing access to articles, charts, news, maps, and videos.

Intergovernmental Panel on Climate Change (IPCC)—www.ipcc.ch

Part of the United Nations, the IPCC assesses the science related to climate change. It researches and publishes periodic reports on the effects of climate change. The reports are often technical, but executive summaries of these provide accessible facts and other information.

National Aeronautics and Space Administration (NASA)—www.climate.nasa.gov

NASA is the premier US space agency. The "Global Climate Change: Vital Signs of the Planet" section of the NASA website provides excellent facts, explanations, articles, graphics, and more on the topic of climate change.

National Snow and Ice Data Center (NSIDC)—www.nsidc.org

The NSIDC researches the world's glaciers, ice fields, snow, and frozen ground (aka the cryosphere), and it studies how the climate affects these frozen realms. In cooperation with NASA satellite data, it creates maps of the changes in arctic ice. The site provides answers to popular questions about ice and glaciers, quick facts about the cryosphere, a primer on Arctic climatology, and lists of resources for further information.

Skeptical Science—www.skepticalscience.com

This educational website concentrates on explaining the science behind climate change without political bias. It presents scientific responses to such arguments as "Earth warming is a natural event." The site includes the latest news on climate science, an interactive timeline of climate history, graphic illustrations of various aspects of climate change, and much more educational information.

Woods Hole Oceanographic Institution (WHOI)—www.whoi.edu

An organization dedicated to ocean research and education, the WHOI presents the latest information on the environment through reports, videos of its ocean expeditions, and stories on the impact of climate change on the world's oceans and aquatic life.

Books

Jeffrey Bennett, *Global Warming Primer: Answering Your Questions About the Science, the Consequences, and the Solutions*. Boulder, CO: Big Kid Science, 2016.

Kerry Emanuel, *What We Know About Climate Change*. Cambridge, MA: MIT Press, 2018.

Joshua S. Goldstein and Staffan A. Qvist, *A Bright Future: How Some Countries Have Solved Climate Change and the Rest Can Follow*. New York: Public Affairs, 2019.

Dahr Jamail, *The End of Ice: Bearing Witness and Finding Meaning in the Path of Climate Disruption*. New York: New, 2019.

Amanda Little, *The Fate of Food: What We'll Eat in a Bigger, Hotter, Smarter World*. New York: Harmony, 2019.

Don Nardo, *Planet Under Siege: Climate Change*. San Diego, CA: ReferencePoint, 2020.

Joseph Romm, *Climate Change: What Everyone Needs to Know*. New York: Oxford University Press, 2018.

Roger A. Sedjo, *Surviving Global Warming: Why Eliminating Greenhouse Gases Isn't Enough*. New York: Prometheus, 2019.

Timothy C. Winegard, *The Mosquito: A Human History of Our Deadliest Predator*. New York: Dutton, 2019.

Internet Sources

Erin Blakemore, "We're Barreling Towards Another Dust Bowl," *Popular Science*, August 19, 2019. www.popsci.com.

Kashmira Gander, "'Our Futures Are at Risk': Meet the Kids Skipping School to Join the Global Climate Strike," *Newsweek*, September 17, 2019. www.newsweek.com.

Lauren Harper, "Glaciers, Ice Sheets, and More: A Primer on the Different Types of Polar Ice," *State of the Planet* (blog), Earth Institute, Columbia University, February 5, 2018. https://blogs .ei.columbia.edu.

Sarah Kaplan and Emily Guskin, "Most American Teens Are Frightened by Climate Change, Poll Finds, and About 1 in 4 Are Taking Action," *Washington Post*, September 16, 2019. www .washingtonpost.com.

World Health Organization, "Climate Change and Health," February 1, 2018. www.who.int.

Young People's Trust for the Environment, "Renewable Energy Fact Sheet." https://ypte.org.uk.

Index

Note: Boldface page numbers indicate illustrations.

African Forest Landscape Restoration Initiative, 59
agriculture
  Amazon rain forest burnings and, 10
  as carbon dioxide emitter, 35–36
  as carbon dioxide "sink," 35
  changing crops grown, 37, 61–62
  crop yields
    growing season and, 34–35
    rainfall and, 36, 37
    temperature and, 33–34, **34**
  droughts and, 17
  Dust Bowl (1930s), 30, 31, **31**
  flooded fields, 36–38
  livestock
    cows, 33, **39**
    as emitter of greenhouse gases, 6
    importance of, 39
    percent of land on Earth devoted to, 32
    rising temperatures and, 40
  mitigation methods, 55
  percent of land on Earth devoted to, 32
  water usage by, 35
air pollution
  concentration of carbon dioxide in air (2019), 55
  ozone levels and health, 46–47
  smog in New Delhi, 44
algae
  coral and, 28, 29
  krill and, 27
Ali, Mohammad, 48
Amazon rain forest, 10–11
American Farm Bureau Federation, 36
American Meteorological Society, 29
American Psychological Association, 50–51
Anchorage, Alaska, 4
anthrogenic, defined, 6
Archer Daniels Midland (ADM), 59
Asparagopsis (seaweed), 33
asthma, 45–47

Bahamas, 11, 13–14
Barrett, Ko, 7
Billion Tree Tsunami, 59
Black Sunday (April 14, 1935), 30
Bramble Cay melomys, extinction of, 28
Bright Future, A (Goldstein and Qvist), 53–54
Burrows, Elvis, 49–50
Bush, George W., 53

Camp Fire (California, 2018), 8, **9,** 10
Carbon Brief (website), 14–15
Carbon Cycle Institute, 35–36
carbon dioxide
  capture
    by agriculture, 35
    geologic sequestration, 59
    "mechanical trees," 59–60
    rain forests, 10
    "sinks," 10, 35, 58–60
  concentration in air (2019), 55
  emissions
    from agriculture, 6, 35–36
    need to cut, 7
    Sweden's reduction, 53–55, 56
  increase in ocean acidification, 27–29
carbon footprints, 62
Carr, Baily, 52
Chicago, 50
China, 55, 57
Cholayil, Gopakumar, 16
cholera, 47–48
chronic obstructive pulmonary disease, 45
cities
  heat waves and, 45
  rising sea levels and coastal, 21–22, **23**
  See also specific cities
civil unrest, 38–39
clean energy sources, 7, 55–57
Climate Central, 12
climate change
  as anthropogenic, 6–7
  described, 5
  weather compared to climate, 5
Climate Change and Land (IPCC), 30–31

coastal cities and rising sea levels, 21–22, **23**
Congressional Research Service, 13
coral, 27–29
corn, 33–34, **34**
Costa Rica, 61–62
costs
    global investment needed to reduce climate change, 11
    of Hurricane Dorian to Bahamas, 11
    to United States
        Camp Fire (California, 2018), 10
        Dust Bowl, 31
        of extreme weather events (2016–2018), 11
        Hurricane Katrina, 11
        natural disasters (2018) to business, 10
        number of acres destroyed by wildfires since 2000, 13
Coumou, Dim, 15
cows, 33, **39**
Cullmann, Johannes, 6
Cunsolo, Ashlee, 51
Currier, Carlyle, 40

deaths
    from air pollution, 46
    from cholera, 47
    from flooding, 16
    heat waves
        Chicago (1995), 50
        as deadliest extreme weather events, 18
        increase in, 45
        Paris (2019), 4
        people most at risk, 18
    from hurricanes, 13
    from mosquitoes/malaria, 41, 42
    from polar bear attacks, 26
Decatur, Illinois, 59
DeLoach, John, 17
desertification, 30–31
Douty, Adam, 13
droughts
    effects on agriculture, 38
    following floods, 16
    increase in longer and more severe, 16–17
    livestock and, 40
    temperature-driven, 38

Zambezi River, 15
Durack, Paul, 17
Dust Bowl (1930s), 30, 31, **31**

Earth
    area covered by ice, 21, 24
    increase in population of, 40
    percent of, covered by water, 20
    percent of land devoted to agriculture, 32
East Africa, 36–38
ecoAmerica, 50–51
electric vehicles, 7
Elsner, James B., 13
endangered species, 25–27, **26**
Epstein, Paul R., 41
extreme weather events, increase in, 14–15

farming. *See* agriculture
"fingerprints," 17
floods
    farmland, 36–38
    Hurricane Harvey, **49**
    India, 16, **17**
    mental effects of, 49–50
    water polluted by, 48
Foerster, Jim, 10
food insecurity
    climate change and
        areas affected, 35
        droughts, 38–39
        population increase, 40
    described, 32
food supply, 33–35, **34**
Forster, Piers, 63
France, 4, **6**, 55
Frank, Leitu, 23
freshwater, percent of Earth's water, 20

Gentine, Pierre, 38
geologic sequestration, 59
Geophysical Fluid Dynamics Laboratory (NASA), 14
glaciers, 19–21, **20**, 24
global climate strike (2019), 52
global warming, 5
Goldman, Lynn, 48
Goldstein, Joshua S., 53–54
Gore, Tim, 32
greenhouse effect, 5

greenhouse gases
    amount of, 5
    effect of, 5
    emissions, 6, 35–36
    major, 5
    methane, 33
    reducing, 53–55
    See also carbon dioxide
Griffen, Blaine, 25
Grundstein, Andrew, 44–45

Hansen, James, 21
health
    air pollution and, 44, 46–47
    community, 50–51
    heat waves and, 43–45, **46**
    mental, 49–50
    mosquitoes, 41–43, **43**
    respiratory, 44, 45–47
    water pollution and, 47–48
heat waves
    Chicago (1995), 50
    global (2019), 4, **6**, 17–18
    health and, 43–45, **46**
Houston, Texas, **49**
human activities, 6–7
hurricanes
    Dorian (2019), 11, 13–14
    effect of climate change on, 12–13,
        14
    Harvey (2017), 11–12, 14, **49**
    Katrina (2005), 11, **12**, 48
hydropower, 15, 56

Ice, Cloud, and Land Elevation
    Satellite-2 (ICESat-2), 24
ice caps, 21, 24
ice sheets, 21, 24
Illinois Industrial Carbon Capture Project,
    59
India
    food insecurity in, 32
    pollution and health, 44
    torrential rains followed by drought in
        Kerala, 16, **17**
Intergovernmental Panel on Climate
    Change (IPCC)
    effect of climate change on agriculture,
        30–31
    ocean warming as cause of increase in
        temperatures, 21

on scope of problem of climate
    change, 7
international agreements, 53
Inuit, 51

Jenouvrier, Stephanie, 27
Jordan, Justin, 36

kärnkraft, 54–55
Kenya, 36–38
Kerala (India), 16, **17**
Kiribati, 60–61, **61**
krill, 27
Kyoto Protocol (1997), 53

Lackner, Klaus, 59–60
Landsat 8, 24
Las Vegas, Nevada, 45
Lawrence Livermore National Laboratory
    (LLNL), 16–17
lightning, 10
livestock
    cows, 33, **39**
    as emitter of greenhouse gases, 6
    importance of, 39
    percent of land on Earth devoted to, 32
    rising temperatures and, 40
Lungu, Edgar, 15

malaria, 41, 42
"mechanical trees," 59–60
Meneses, Evan, 52
methane, 33
Mgogwana, Yola, 52
Minnis, Hubert, 14
mosquitoes, 41–43, **43**

National Aeronautics and Space
    Administration (NASA)
    concentration of carbon dioxide in air
        (2019), 55
    hottest years since 1880, 5
    tracking of melting ice on Earth by, 24
National Clean Air Program (India), 44
National Geographic Society, 42
National Hurricane Center, 14
National Oceanic and Atmospheric
    Administration, 14
Neira, Maria, 46
Nepal, 37
New Delhi, India, 44

New Orleans, Louisiana, **12,** 48
New York City, 22, **23,** 52
Nix, Steve, 10
Norway, 56
no-till farming, 55

oceans
    effects of increase in acidity of, 27–29
    effects of sea ice melting on, 21,
        25–26, **26,** 27
    increase in temperature of and
        global temperature rise, 21
        hurricanes, 12–13
        krill and penguins, 27
    rising levels of
        animals and, 28
        coastal cities and, 21–22, **23**
        ice melting and, 21
        Kiribati and, 60–61, **61**
Okjökull (Ok Glacier, Iceland), 19
ozone, 46–47

Pakistan, 59
Paradise, California, 8, **9**
Paris, France, 4, **6**
Paris Agreement (2015), 53
penguins, 26–27
PLOS ONE (journal), 10
polar bears, 25–26, **26**
population, increase in, 40
positive feedback loop, 38
Pottle, Derrick, 51
Poudel, Madan, 37
protests, global climate strike (2019),
    52

Qvist, Staffan A., 53–54

rainfall
    changes in patterns, 9, 37
    increase in, and mosquitoes, 43, **43**
    increase in extreme, 15–16
    timing of, and crop yields, 36, 37
    See also hurricanes
rain forests, 10–11
reforestation, 58–59
renewable energy sources, 55–57, **57**
Reser, Joseph, 49
Rice, Doyle, 18
Rigolet, Canada, 51
Rugalema, Gabriel, 37–38

Saha, Shubhayu, 45
Scheelbeek, Pauline, 34
seawalls, 61
seaweed, 33
Sharma, Salil, 44
Siegel, Anna, 52
Sigurdsson, Oddur, 19
"sinks"
    agriculture as, 35
    "mechanical trees" as, 59–60
    rain forests as, 10
    reforestation and, 58–59
Sione, Enna, 24
smog, 44, 46
solar power, 56, 57, **57**
solutions
    geologic sequestration, 59
    global climate strike (2019) demanding,
        52
    importance of international
        cooperation, 63
    mitigation
        agricultural methods, 55
        international agreements, 53
        reducing carbon footprints, 62
        Sweden, 53–55, 56
    renewable energy sources, 55–57, **57**
    "sinks"
        agriculture as, 35
        "mechanical trees" as, 59–60
        rain forests as, 10
        reforestation and, 58–59
    Thunberg and, 58
South America, fires in Amazon rain
    forest, 10
Sweden, 53–55, 56
Syria, 38–39

Taalas, Petteri, 5
teenagers, feelings about climate change,
    54
Tehmasip, Muhammad, 59
temperatures
    heat waves
        Chicago (1995), 50
        global (2019), 4, **6,** 17–18
        health during, 43–45, **46**
    hottest years since 1880, 5
    rising
        changing crops grown, 61–62
        crop yields and, 33–34, **34**

diseases and, 42, 48
livestock and, 40
ocean warming as cause of, 21
ozone levels and, 47
rainfall patterns and, 38
Third National Climate Assessment
report (US Global Change Research
Program), 14
Thunberg, Greta, 58
Time (magazine), 58
tree rings, 16–17
Trouet, Valerie, 38
Trump, Donald and Paris Agreement, 53
Tuvalu, 22–24

UN Climate Action Summit, 58
Union of Concerned Scientists, 16, 47
United Nations Environment Programme,
47
United States
costs
Camp Fire (California, 2018), 10
Dust Bowl, 31
extreme weather events (2016–
2018), 11
Hurricane Katrina, 11
natural disasters (2018) to business,
10
number of acres destroyed since
2000 due to wildfires, 13
Department of Agriculture, 32
Department of Energy, 56, 57
droughts, 38
Dust Bowl (1930s), 30, 31, **31**
farmlands flooded, 36
food insecurity in, 32
Geological Survey, 22, 59
geologic sequestration, 59
Global Change Research Program, 14
heat waves in, 44, 45, **46**, 50
ice melting and coastal cities in, 22, **23**
importance of ocean industries to
economy, 29
Kyoto Protocol, 53
nuclear power in, 55
Paris Agreement, 53
percent of adults worried about climate
change in, 49
solar power, 56, **57**
wind farms, 56

University of California, Davis, 33

vector-borne diseases, 42–43
Victoria Falls (Zambezi River), 15

water
agricultural use of, 35
percent of Earth covered by, 20
polluted, 47–48
rising temperatures and diseases borne
by, 48
See also droughts; floods; hurricanes;
rainfall
weather, compared to climate, 5
Werpy, Todd, 59
wildfires
Camp Fire (California, 2018), 8, **9**, 10
climate change and conditions for,
9–10
costs, 10
number of US acres destroyed since
2000, 13
Williams, Park, 9
wind farms, 56
winds
tropical storms and, 11, 12–13
wildfires and, 8
Wismayer, Henry, 25
Woods Hole Oceanographic Institution
(WHOI), 27
World Bank, 35
World Economic Forum, 56
World Health Organization (WHO)
chronic obstructive pulmonary disease,
45
mosquitoes as cause of human deaths,
41
population at risk for malaria, 42

Yale Program on Climate Change
Communication, 49
York, Geoff, 26
Young, Leslie, 42

Zambezi River, 15
Zambia, 15
Zarrilli, Daniel, 22
Zelaya, Sergio, 35
Zimbabwe, 15
zooxanthellae, 28, 29

Craig E. Blohm has written numerous books and magazine articles for young readers. He and his wife, Desiree, reside in Tinley Park, Illinois.